WAFFEN-SS PANZERS

EASTERN FRONT

Tim Ripley

Windmill Books Ltd
9-17 St. Alban's Place
London
N1 0NX
UK
www.windmillbooks.co.uk

© 2015 Brown Bear Books Limited

All rights reserved. No part of this publication may be reproduced, stored in a retrieval system, or transmitted in any form or by any means electronic, mechanical, photocopying, recording, or otherwise, without the prior permission in writing of the copyright holder.

You must not circulate this book in any other binding or cover and you must impose this same condition on any acquirer.

The information in this book is true and complete to the best of our knowledge. All recommendations are made without any guarantee on the part of the author or publisher, who also disclaim any liability incurred in connection with the use of this data or specified details.

We recognize that some words, model names and designations, for example, mentioned herein are the property of the trademark holder. We use them for identification purposes only. This is not an official publication.

The maps contain elements adapted from OpenStreetMap map data, © OpenStreetMap contributors, licensed under the Creative Commons Attribution ShareAlike 2.0 License.

ISBN 978-1-78121-226-0

Editor: Peter Darman
Maps: Ben Hollingum

All photographs courtesy of the Robert Hunt Library.

Contents

Key to Maps 4
List of Maps 5
Captions 6
Acknowledgements 7

Introduction: Hitler's Guard 8
Chapter 1: Winter Tempest 14
Chapter 2: Waffen-SS – Panzer Elite 24
Chapter 3: Kharkov 43
Chapter 4: Kursk 73
Chapter 5: Death Ride of the *Totenkopf* 114
Chapter 6: The Führer's Fire Brigade 130
Chapter 7: Death on the Dnieper 145
Chapter 8: Kessel Battles 158
Chapter 9: Holding the Line 175
Chapter 10: Spring Awakening 185
Chapter 11: The Bitter End 205

Appendices 210
Bibliography 231

Key to Maps

Military units – types

- ARMOUR
- INFANTRY
- ARMY GROUP
- CAVALRY
- AIRBORNE INFANTRY
- MOTORIZED / MECHANIZED INFANTRY

Military units – size

- XXXXX ARMY GROUP
- XXXX ARMY
- XXX CORPS
- XX DIVISION
- X BRIGADE
- III REGIMENT
- II BATTALION
- I COMPANY

Military unit colours

- RED ARMY (SOVIET UNION)
- AXIS FORCES (NAZI GERMANY, ITALY, HUNGARY, ROMANIA)

Military movement

- ATTTACK/ADVANCE (IN NATIONAL COLOURS)
- RETREAT (IN NATIONAL COLOURS)

Geographical symbols

- ROAD
- URBAN AREA
- RIVER
- RAILWAY

Military units – name

The upper number is the unit's official designation. The designation of corps-level formations is usually written in Roman numerals. The lower letters show any special characteristics the unit has.

SS — Waffen-SS
Gds — Guards (Red Army elite units)
Sh — Shock (A Red Army formation intended to spearhead major offensives)
OG — Operational group
(Romanian) — Country names in brackets indicate a foreign formation fighting under the overall command of another nation.

List of Maps

The German Summer Offensive:
24 July–18 November 1942 17
Operation Uranus: 19–30 November 1942 19
The Second Battle of Kharkov: 9–20 February 1943 45
The Third Battle of Kharkov: 5–23 March 1943 60
The Battle of Kursk: Soviet defensive belts 76
The Battle of Kursk: German Plans 85
The Battle of Kursk: Southern front, 4–7 July 1943 96
The Battle of Kursk: Southern front, 9–11 July 1943 99
The Battle of Kursk: Prokhorovka, 12 July 1943 105
The Mius Bridgehead: 30 July 1943 123
The Fourth Battle of Kharkov: 3–8 August 1943 134
The Fourth Battle of Kharkov: 11–12 August 1943 138
The Attack on Radomyschl: 15–21 August 1943 149
The Attack on Radomyschl:
26 November–23 December 1943 153
The Breakthrough at Kirovograd: 11–16 January 1944 161
The Cherkassy Pocket:
Relief attempts, 16–20 February 1944 166
The Kamenets-Podolsk Pocket:
Situation on 4 March 1944 171
Operation Bagration: 23 June–28 July 1944 179
Operation Spring Awakening: 6–15 March 1945 193
The Vienna Offensive: 16 March–15 April 1945 194

Captions

Introduction: This dramatic publicity shot, taken on the Eastern Front, shows a *Totenkopf* Division Panzer IV advancing through a smokescreen.

Chapter 1. A StuG III assault gun operating in the snows of Southern Russia, late 1942.

Chapter 2. A group of Panzer IV tanks from II SS Panzer Corps at a marshalling area near Kursk, July 1943.

Chapter 3. A Waffen-SS MG 42 machine gun team covers the advance of a group of infantry during an assault on a Soviet-held factory complex on the outskirts of Kharkov.

Chapter 4. A *Das Reich* Division Tiger I tank moves forward at Kursk as Waffen-SS panzergrenadiers consolidate their positions on the exposed Russian steppe.

Chapter 5. Heavily-armed *Das Reich* Division panzergrenadiers prior to mounting up on their SdKfz 251 halftracks for a combined tank and infantry attack.

Chapter 6. A German sentry watches a road in southern Russia from a foxhole dug amidst the wreckage of a failed Red Army offensive.

Chapter 7. A group of German soldiers, dressed in full winter uniforms, wade through waist deep snowdrifts alongside a Panzer IV.

Chapter 8. Panzer IV's loaded with panzergrenadiers disappear into the winter gloom on their way to join the relief force fighting its way to the Cherkassy Pocket.

Chapter 9. German infantry walk through the snow beside an armoured column during the retreat from the Dneiper.

Chapter 10. The enormous bulk of a Tiger II ('King Tiger') tank on the streets of Budapest in 1945.

Chapter 11. The streets of Berlin, April 1945. The mangled wreckage of military vehicles and the unburied dead reveal the city's immediate past.

Acknowledgements

This book is dedicated to the heroes of the Red Army's XVIII and XXIX Tank Corps, who first engaged II SS Panzer Corps at Prokhorovka in the titanic tank battle on 12 July 1943. For the next two years, brave Soviet tank crews of these two fine units would be in the vanguard of driving Hitler's Waffen-SS panzer elite back into the heart of the Third Reich, so freeing Europe of Nazi tyranny for good.

The author would like to thank the following people for their help during the researching and writing of this study. Neil Tweedie of *The Daily Telegraph*, for his unique insights into Nazi mentality; the Imperial War Museum records staff in London for their help with research into German World War II documents; the British Army Staff College, Camberley, for allowing me access to rare German World War II records in their possession; Stewart Frazer for proof-reading my text; Pete Darman, of Windmill Books, for at last giving me the opportunity to fulfil my long-held ambition to write about the Eastern Front; and finally, Mr McAlpine, my history teacher, for inspiring my interest in World War II.

Tim Ripley

Introduction
HITLER'S GUARD

The ethos of the Waffen-SS and the war on the Eastern Front.

The Eastern Front was the decisive theatre of operations during World War II. The pivotal point came in mid-1943, when the Red Army and Nazi Germany massed the largest tank forces in the history of modern warfare for a titanic clash of armour. At the Battle of Kursk in July 1943, millions of troops and thousands of tanks clashed in an epic engagement. The Red Army's defences held and Adolf Hitler's panzer armies were stopped in their tracks. Over the next 21 months, having gained the strategic initiative, the mighty Red Army surged forward into the heart of the Führer's Thousand Year Reich.

Standing in the way of the Russians was an increasingly beleaguered and battle-weary Wehrmacht, its divisions under strength and its reserves largely spent. When crises threatened, Hitler turned to the elite panzer divisions of the Waffen-SS. Time and again they were thrown into desperate holding actions and counterattacks to plug gaps in Germany's Eastern Front. As a result, they soon became known as the Führer's "Fire Brigade". As the war progressed, these actions became more forlorn until even the die-hard Waffen-SS commanders could see that their cause was lost.

This book tells the story of the actions of the Waffen-SS *Leibstandarte, Das Reich, Totenkopf, Wiking, Hitlerjugend, Hohenstaufen* and *Frundsberg* Divisions on the Eastern Front between 1943 and 1945. These include their dramatic successes during the German counteroffensive after the surrender at Stalingrad, along with the preparations for the Kursk Offensive. The key role in Operation Citadel, the codename of the German attack, of the Waffen-SS panzers is explained using newly available original sources which throw fresh light on the course of the battle.

During the eight months after the failure at Kursk, the Waffen-SS panzers were deployed again and again to try to prevent Field Marshal Erich von Manstein's Army Group South from being overwhelmed by thousands of Soviet tanks. In battle after battle, the Waffen-SS destroyed hundreds of T-34s, only to encounter scores of new Red Army tank brigades on the winter battlefields of the Ukraine.

While the bulk of the Waffen-SS panzer force was pulled back from the East to counter the D-Day landings in France in June 1944, the *Totenkopf* and *Wiking* Divisions remained behind to help defend Poland during the summer and autumn of 1944. After the failed Ardennes Offensive, Hitler ordered the Waffen-SS panzers to mass in Hungary during January 1945 in a bid to break the Soviet siege of Budapest. The subsequent offensive was the death ride of the Waffen-SS panzers, and within a few weeks the morale of the once proud elite armoured force was broken for good. Shattered, they headed west to escape Soviet vengeance.

In their brief existence, the Waffen-SS panzer divisions established for themselves a reputation as some of the most formidable formations in the history of armoured warfare. While some historians have tried to attribute their battlefield success to their abundant supplies of the best tanks and other material, this is a simplistic analysis. The Waffen-SS panzer divisions may have been new to armoured warfare in early 1943, but their men learnt fast and were soon able to execute many complicated and difficult battlefield manoeuvres.

The key to their success was undoubtedly their unique *esprit de corps*, which enabled them to absorb thousands of casualties and still keep on fighting in the face of overwhelming odds. Time after time, Waffen-SS divisions were rebuilt after suffering sometimes in the region of 75 percent casualty rates. This amazing feat was due to a number of factors. Principally, it was down to the dynamic leadership of a cadre of junior and senior commanders. Key Waffen-SS company, battalion and regimental commanders were all in their late twenties or early thirties. These men were almost all fanatical pre-war Nazi Party members who believed in the racial superiority of the German "master race", and many were protégés of Hitler himself or other senior members of the Nazi Party.

Waffen-SS officers were a breed apart. They were charismatic and vigorous, generating loyalty and unwavering obedience from subordinates. At the same time, they made a point of not displaying fear or nerves in public. Most had been wounded several times in battle, but they managed to generate an aura of indestructibility. No matter how many tight scrapes they got into, these men still made their troops feel that no harm would come to them as long as they stuck close and did not waver. In Nazi Germany, being an officer in the Waffen-SS brought with it immense power and privileges. Even junior Waffen-SS officers held the power of life and death over the civilian populations of occupied countries, and they were not afraid to use that power if the occasion merited. The mere sight of an SS uniform was enough to turn even the most defiant Russian civilian into a cowed slave. Away from the frontline, Waffen-SS officers and soldiers lived the high life. Their Führer may have been a tee-total vegetarian, but his elite troops knew how to live life to the full. Nazi propaganda broadcasts, newsreels and magazines turned Waffen-SS officers into celebrities, which further fuelled their egos. The result was a heady mix of super confidence, verging on arrogance.

The Waffen-SS panzer leaders learned their trade during the Blitzkrieg years of victories in 1939–41, so that by the spring of 1943 they were battle hardened from earlier campaigns in the West and Russia. Key commanders moved up the ladder of promotion between the various divisions, and so got to know each other well. Although this meant rivalry, it also resulted in senior commanders knowing their subordinates' strengths or foibles before units entered battle. This meant that, in the heat of battle, Waffen-SS panzer units could be quickly combined or placed under the command of different divisions with the minimum of disruption or confusion. The ability to regroup at short notice on a battlefield to meet a new threat, or begin a new offensive, was often a decisive factor in bringing victory. Thus by the summer of 1943, the Waffen-SS panzer divisions had grown into well-oiled professional fighting machines.

The elite Waffen-SS divisions soon proved themselves to be skilled practitioners of armoured warfare. Their aggressive character and free-wheeling style lent itself to success in fast-moving tank battles. Often battle would turn on a few critical decisions or engagements, in which a quick-witted Waffen-SS panzer commander would see an opportunity and seize it. The strictly regimented Red Army, in which individual initiative was stifled, could not cope with such tactics. A vital factor in the success of the Waffen-SS panzer divisions was their ability to deploy the combined-arms *kampfgruppe* (battle group), which brought together tanks, artillery, mechanized infantry, combat engineers and reconnaissance teams under a single commander.

A common trait among Waffen-SS commanders, and an important ingredient for success, was utter ruthlessness. Once given a battlefield mission, Waffen-SS officers were rarely deflected from their task. Neither friends nor foes were spared in the pursuit of victory. A side effect of this was their treatment of prisoners and civilians. Although some apologists for the Waffen-SS have tried to portray them as simple soldiers who strictly followed the rules of war, time and again Waffen-SS commanders would order the execution of prisoners or civilians who were hindering an advance or obstructing other activities. In the West, many of these atrocities have come to light as result of war crimes trials; but in the East the crimes of the Waffen-SS remain largely anonymous. The most famous of these occurred in the occupation of the Ukrainian city of Kharkov during the spring of 1943, which saw some 10,000 civilians and prisoners of war perish at the hand of vengeful Waffen-SS troops.

To Waffen-SS men, and according to National Socialist ideology, their Soviet opponents were *untermensch*, or subhumans, whose lives were worthless. Therefore the rules of war enshrined in the Geneva Convention did not apply. This attitude was reciprocated by the Red Army. Waffen-SS men were regarded as prized prisoners by the Soviets. To be caught by the Red Army wearing SS runes could mean a bullet in the back of the neck. Capturing and killing Waffen-SS men was seen by Communist Party Commissars as a means of striking at the ideological heart of the Nazi regime. Desecration of Waffen-SS graves was also common in Russia – mercy was in short supply on the Eastern Front.

In the final analysis, while the Waffen-SS were tough and skilful soldiers, this was not enough to turn the tide on the Eastern Front in the face of overwhelming Soviet manpower and equipment resources. The Waffen-SS panzer divisions could not be everywhere, and by early 1945 even their battle-hardened leadership realized the game was up. They refused to go down fighting in a modern-day Götterdämmerung, and sought to find the best surrender terms for themselves and their men.

Chapter 1
WINTER TEMPEST

Stalingrad and the threat to Army Group South, 1942–43.

Southern Russia in December 1942 was gripped by winter. Russia's flat plains, or steppes, were white as far as the eye could see thanks to heavy coverings of snow. The temperature rarely rose above freezing during daylight hours, and at night it regularly dropped to minus 40 degrees centigrade. The sun did not rise until mid-morning, and even then thick cloud meant every day was grey and gloomy. This matched the mood of the German soldiers on the Eastern Front.

The previous month, seven Soviet armies had launched a counteroffensive against the Wehrmacht's Sixth Army at

WINTER TEMPEST

Stalingrad, trapping its 220,000 men inside a pocket along the frozen banks of the River Volga. Six months before, these men had been the spearhead of Operation Blue. Adolf Hitler hoped this offensive would knock the Soviet Union out of the war for good by seizing its strategically crucial Caucasus oil wells, bringing the Red Army's tanks to a grinding halt through lack of fuel. Two German army groups, led by nine panzer divisions and seven motorized divisions equipped with some 800 tanks, at first swept all before them. Tens of thousands of Russian soldiers were trapped in pockets as German panzers manoeuvred effortlessly across the featureless steppe. The First Panzer Army, with the Waffen-SS *Wiking* Motorized Division in its vanguard, swept into the Caucasus seizing the Maikop oil field and then headed hundreds of kilometres southwards towards the region now know as Chechnya. The city of Stalingrad was the key. If the Germans took it they could block off the Caucasus from the rest of Russia. However, if the Soviets held the city, they could keep the oil flowing and retain a springboard for a westward counteroffensive to trap the German forces moving south into the Caucasus.

By the autumn, fanatical resistance by Red Army troops in Stalingrad had brought the German eastward advance to a halt. Vicious street battles sucked in German division after division, until the bulk of the Sixth Army's combat troops were fighting in an area of only a few score square kilometres. No matter how hard General Friedrich Paulus drove his tired troops forward into the alleys and ruined factories of Stalingrad, the Soviet defenders refused to give up the fight. The Sixth Army's commander loyally followed his Führer's orders to fight on in the devastated city, despite warning signs that the Soviets were massing forces elsewhere for a huge counteroffensive.

WAFFEN-SS PANZERS: EASTERN FRONT

On 19 November, the Red Army launched Operation Saturn. Hundreds of tanks surged forward across the thinly held lines of the Romanian Third Army, which had the task of holding hundreds of kilometres of front to the north of Stalingrad. The Romanians had no modern antitank weapons, and within hours they had either fled westwards, died in the snow or surrendered. The following day, another Soviet tank force broke through the Romanian Fourth Army, to the south of the Sixth Army. A day later the arms of the two Russian pincers met to the west of Stalingrad, trapping the hapless Paulus and his troops in the city. The 100 or so German Panzer III and 30 Panzer IV tanks of the three badly weakened panzer divisions in what was now known grandly as "Fortress Stalingrad" were unable to challenge the 635 Russian tanks ringing the Sixth Army, because Hitler refused to allow them to be redeployed to counter the new threat. Any sort of relief would have to come from outside the pocket.

The immediate German reserve, some 80km (50 miles) to the west of Stalingrad, was the 22nd Panzer Division, but most of its 22 Panzer III and 11 Panzer IV tanks were useless because rodents had eaten into their power cables. In any case, it was soon surrounded by marauding Russian tanks and only just managed to escape westwards after suffering heavy casualties. The division was disbanded soon afterwards.

German forces in southern Russia had to react quickly to avoid being overrun by Red Army columns that were fanning out westwards from Stalingrad. Supply dumps and Luftwaffe airbases were hastily evacuated and small ad hoc kampfgruppen were formed to defend an improvised defensive line along the frozen River Chir, to allow a rescue force for Stalingrad to be assembled. This desperate last line of resistance also protected

WINTER TEMPEST

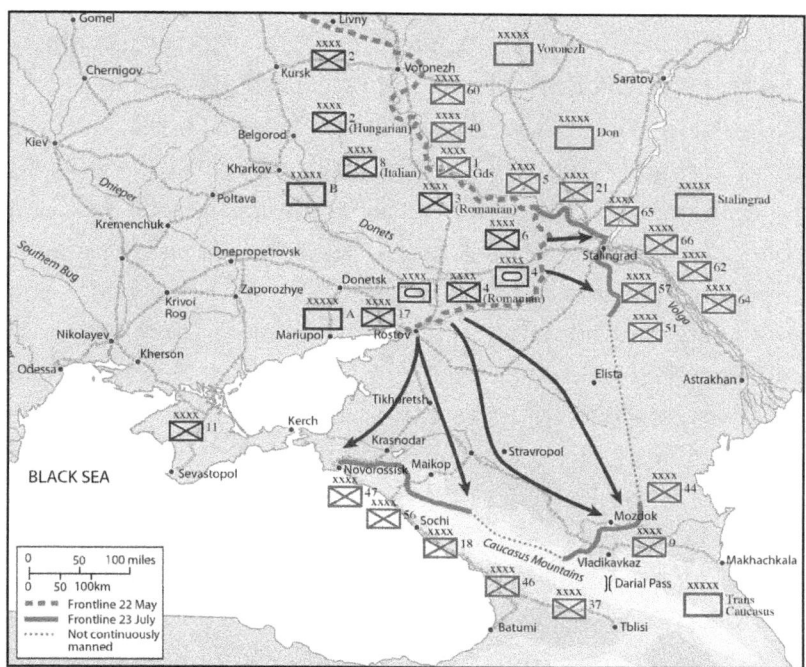

The German Summer Offensive: 24 July–18 November 1942

the vital Morosowskaja and Tatsinskaja airfields, which were to be used by the Luftwaffe to fly in supplies to the Sixth Army after Hermann Göring, head of the Luftwaffe, rashly promised that his airmen could fly in the 508 tonnes (500 tons) of supplies a day needed to keep the troops in Stalingrad fighting.

The man given the job of saving the Stalingrad garrison was Field Marshal Erich von Manstein. He was considered the best operational level commander in the Wehrmacht, and was an expert at armoured warfare. In 18 months of action on the Eastern Front, he had developed an uncannily accurate "feel" for when Soviet offensives would run out of steam. Like a cunning chess player, he was able to look several moves ahead and build plans for devastating counterattacks.

Manstein set up the headquarters for his newly formed Army Group Don on 27 November, and began calling in all available panzer divisions for the Stalingrad rescue mission, codenamed Operation Winter Tempest. A simultaneous breakout plan was developed for the Sixth Army under the codename Thunderclap. The trapped army, however, only had enough fuel for its remaining tanks to strike 32km (20 miles) westwards so everything depended on the rescue force punching through the Russian lines, virtually up to outskirts of Stalingrad. Two fresh panzer divisions were to be mustered for the operation from France and northern Russia, along with a pair of panzer divisions drafted from the southern Caucasus front.

Out on the freezing steppe, Manstein's grand plans had to be turned into reality by small groups of cold, tired and hungry men. Surviving the winter cold was just as much a challenge as keeping the Russians at bay. The key battles were fought not to win the generals some "line on a map", but to control precious shelter. A unit left out in the open at night could die in its tracks. Unlike the year before outside Moscow, the Wehrmacht was now prepared for the winter and special warm clothing had been issued. Even with this equipment, however, soldiers could not spend more than half an hour outside shelter on guard duty at night without suffering fatal frostbite or exposure, while vehicles and heavy weapons had to be kept running and maintained 24 hours a day to stop them freezing solid. In the East during the winter, one of the most important pieces of

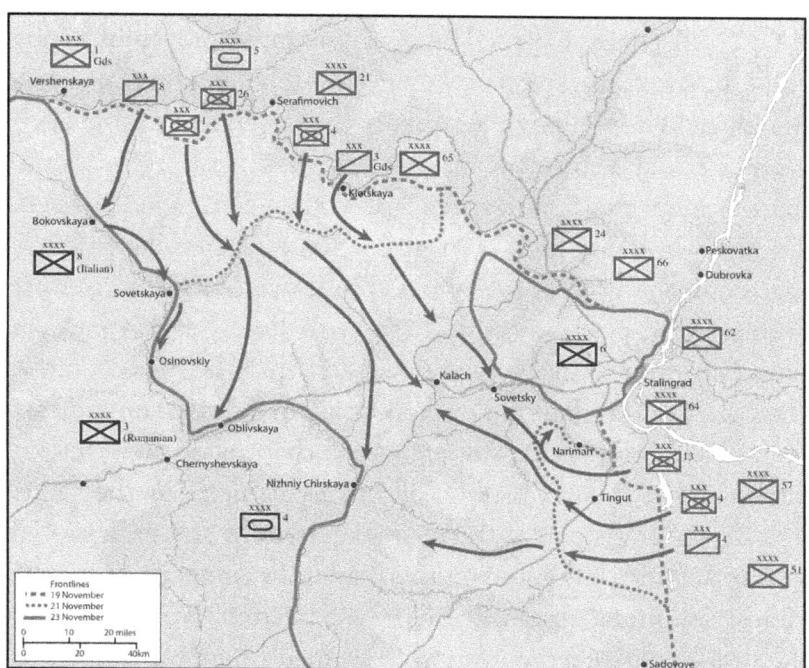

Operation Uranus: 19–30 November 1942

equipment in the Wehrmacht's arsenal was its field kitchens. The delivery of hot food to frontline positions did a lot to sustain morale in truly desperate conditions, and kept men fighting beyond normal levels of endurance. Violent snowstorms could engulf units for days on end, preventing any kind of movement. One of the few benefits of the Russian winter was that it froze the rivers and streams that criss-crossed the steppe, allowing the panzers to manoeuvre freely in much the same way as they did in the North African desert.

It took over a week for the first reinforcements to reach the Chir Front, when the 58 Panzer III and six Panzer IV tanks of the 11th Panzer Division were placed under the command of

XXXXVIII Panzer Corps. The division's tanks moved in a long column across the steppe to their assembly area just behind a weakly held front along the banks of the frozen River Chir. For a week it would be the only combat-ready tank unit in the sector, but was in no position to strike eastwards to Stalingrad by itself. The frontline was held by a mixed force of German infantry and Luftwaffe ground personnel. The Soviets were constantly probing these positions in strength, with almost daily attacks in tank corps strength. On every occasion that the Soviets broke through, the 11th Panzer Division would mobilize its tanks to set up a blocking position. Panzers would then manoeuvre on the flanks of the Soviets, picking off enemy vehicles by the score. The division was one of the most experienced and professional in the Wehrmacht, but even this could not compensate for the almost unlimited resources of the Red Army. For every tank the division knocked out another seemed to appear to take its place, while there were no replacements for lost German tanks. Without rest or relief, it was only a matter of time before the 11th Panzer Division would have to retreat or be destroyed.

On 10 December 1942, LVII Panzer Corps was ready to strike eastwards from its improvised forward base at Kotelnikovo towards Stalingrad. Fresh from France, the 6th Panzer Division led the offensive with its 100 Panzer III and 24 Panzer IV tanks. The already understrength 17th and 23rd Panzer Divisions were brought up from the Caucasus in support. The 17th Panzer was able to muster 30 Panzer IIIs and 18 Panzer IVs, while the 23rd could only scrape together 27 Panzer IIIs and eight Panzer IVs. The men of the three panzer divisions knew they were the last hope for the trapped Sixth Army, and they threw themselves forward with great *élan*. In the space of a week, the 200 tanks of

WINTER TEMPEST

LVII Panzer Corps broke through the Soviet front and pushed forward 160km (100 miles). Using classic panzer tactics, they dodged and weaved their way past scores of Red Army defensive positions. Luftwaffe tank-busting aircraft flew overhead, strafing enemy tank columns, and opening the way for the panzer divisions to push to within 48km (30 miles) of Stalingrad on 20 December. A massive Russian attack far to the north on 16 December broke through the Italian Eighth Army's front, and Soviet armour headed for Rostov, threatening to cut off all the German forces in the Caucasus. To counter this threat, Manstein had to detach the 6th Panzer Division to move north to seal the front. This was the decisive move of the campaign, because now LVII Panzer Corps lacked the strength to punch through to Stalingrad. For five days the now-depleted rescue force held onto to its bridgehead over the River Aksay in the face of furious Soviet attacks.

Hundreds of T-34 tanks at a time were thrown into battle each day by the Soviets before they were knocked out. Inside the pocket, Paulus refused to order Thunderclap. He perhaps did not realize that there were no more panzer reserves available if LVII Panzer Corps failed, or maybe he feared his starving troops were not up to fighting on the open steppe. Whatever the reason the moment was lost. After a huge Soviet attack on its bridgehead on 24 December, LVII Panzer Corps could hold out no more. Two days later it was ordered to fall back on Kotelnikovo. It left behind almost all its tanks and thousands of dead. The 17th Panzer Division could only muster one antitank gun and eight operational tanks. Battalions were reduced to a few hundred men able to fight. Every battalion commander was either dead or wounded. The German Army's panzer divisions were being bled white.

Meanwhile, as the 6th and 11th Panzer Divisions of XXXXVIII Panzer Corps moved westwards to plug the gap in the front created by the collapse of the Italians, they surprised a Red Army guards tank corps that had just seized a Luftwaffe airfield at Tatsinskaya. The two veteran German divisions trapped the Russians between armoured pincers, neutralizing the threat to Rostov, for the moment.

The frontline only held for a matter of days before the Soviets were attacking again. XXXXVIII Panzer Corps stood firm, but all around chaos and confusion reigned. Even the arrival of the 7th Panzer Division from France with 105 Panzer III and 20 Panzer IV tanks was not enough to stabilize the front. At the end of December, Hitler gave Manstein permission to withdraw from the Caucasus, freeing up the First Panzer Army with its 3rd Panzer Division, 16th and 26th Motorized Divisions and the Waffen-SS *Wiking* Division for action farther north. The Führer, however, insisted that the 13th Panzer Division stay in the Caucasus to hold the Kuban Peninsula. As for the other divisions, they still had to travel several hundred kilometres north before their 70 or so tanks could help Manstein.

The 11th Panzer Division had to fight a determined rearguard action to the east of Rostov in mid-January to allow the First Panzer Army to move northwards, into the Ukraine itself.

Through December and into January 1943, the Sixth Army struggled to survive in Stalingrad. Within hours of the failure of Operation Winter Tempest, the Red Army launched a series of massive offensives aimed at destroying the Sixth Army once and for all. Huge rocket and artillery barrages slammed into the German positions. Lack of fuel meant that the few remaining panzers could not launch a counterattack. By this time the

100,000 or so German soldiers now alive in the pocket were so frozen and starving that they were in no position to move out of their improvised bunkers in the ruins of Stalingrad. Göring's much-vaunted airlift was barely able to fly in 101 tonnes (100 tons) of supplies a day, and the Soviet advances westwards reduced this to a trickle as they rolled up the Luftwaffe's network of forward airfields one by one. The Luftwaffe was, however, able to bring out 30,000 wounded Germans. The airlift was put out of action for good on 22 January when the Soviets overran the last German-held airfield in the pocket.

Despite the steady stream of bad news from southern Russia, Hitler was still optimistic that the situation could be redeemed. On 31 December 1942, he ordered I SS Panzer Corps to move from France to Kharkov in the eastern Ukraine to set up a base for a new relief effort towards Stalingrad. While Manstein was pleased to be getting new reinforcements, the idea that three Waffen-SS divisions could push 560km (350 miles) eastwards by themselves to rescue the Sixth Army was considered to be one of the Führer's wilder ideas.

On 24 January 1943, the Russians began their final offensive against "Fortress Stalingrad". Within a week they had overrun what was left of the Sixth Army. Hitler now promoted Paulus in the hope that he would commit suicide rather than suffer the dishonour of being the first ever German field marshal to surrender. In a rare act of defiance to his Führer, Paulus emerged with his staff from his bunker under a bombed-out department store and surrendered on 31 January. A day later the last pocket of German resistance in the city surrendered. Some 91,000 Germans were marched into Soviet captivity. Less than 5000 survived more than a few months as prisoners of Stalin.

Chapter 2
WAFFEN-SS – PANZER ELITE

The hardware and organization of the SS armoured divisions.

As the German Sixth Army was fighting for its life in the ruins of Stalingrad, in occupied France a heavily armed panzer corps was being formed from Waffen-SS units. Soon it would be loaded onto hundreds of trains and sent east to turn back the advancing Red Army.

Adolf Hitler's mistrust of the German Army had grown as the war dragged on. His arguments with senior army generals during the failed offensive against Moscow in the winter of 1941 had convinced him that a politically reliable combat force was needed if the Third Reich was to prevail in the titanic struggle with Stalin's Russia on the Eastern Front. The loyalty and obedience of the Waffen-SS to the cause of Nazism would ensure success in battle, or so the Führer thought. In May 1942, he ordered the formation of a Waffen-SS corps headquarters that was to command the Leibstandarte, Das Reich and Totenkopf Divisions. They were to be refitted after suffering heavy casualties in Russia during the previous winter. By the summer plans had advanced apace, and the Führer now wanted his prized divisions to be equipped as panzergrenadier divisions.

All through the summer and into the autumn, new recruits and new equipment poured into the Waffen-SS bases in occupied France, where the corps was being prepared for action. Here, the three divisions and the corps staff were moulded into fighting units. This was a frantic time for the cadre of Waffen-SS veterans who had to rebuild their shattered units, while at the same time accepting new types of tanks, armoured cars, halftracks, antitank weapons and artillery. The tough training regime was interrupted in November 1942, when the Waffen-SS divisions were used to spearhead the occupation of Vichy France, after the Allied landings in North Africa led to the collapse of the pro-German regime. The exercise only served to show how much work was needed to prepare the divisions for action, as bottlenecks formed and units became disorganized. Once they returned to their bases, the training intensity was redoubled.

Gone were the days when the Waffen-SS only accepted volunteers who had passed rigorous fitness and ideological tests. Tens of thousands of Labour Service draftees, policemen, concentration camp guards and assorted misfits now had to be turned into elite combat soldiers. The officer ranks of the new Waffen-SS panzer force had to learn how to coordinate large numbers of tanks in battle, as well as all the skills necessary to keep tens of thousands of men supplied with all the tools of mobile warfare. As the news from Stalingrad grew worse, it became clear to the Waffen-SS veterans that they would soon be heading east again.

The Waffen-SS had its origins in a small bodyguard squad – the SS, *Schutz Staffel* (Protection Squad) – created by Hitler during the 1920s to fight his political rivals in the back streets of Munich. When the Nazi Party came to power in 1933, Hitler immediately set about creating a Praetorian Guard from his most loyal supporters. They were to be a small, elite force, distinct from the Nazi Party's paramilitary Stormtrooper, or SA, militia which boasted tens of thousands of members throughout Germany. Eventually known as the *Leibstandarte Adolf Hitler* (Bodyguard Regiment Adolf Hitler), the squad had soon grown into 200 well-armed men who were fanatically loyal to their Führer. Hitler came to view the SA as a potential rival power base, and within months of coming to power he had purged its leadership of disloyal elements. The *Leibstandarte* moved with ruthless efficiency to arrest the SA leadership during June 1934, in a coup d'état known as the "Night of the Long Knives". Over several days the rogue SA leaders were murdered. The favoured method was a pistol shot to the back of the neck. Several senior SS men who would later rise to prominence in the Waffen-SS played a prominent role in this massacre, including Josef "Sepp" Dietrich and Theodore Eicke.

During the remainder of the 1930s, the SS grew into a massive organization which was, in effect, a parallel state, answering only to Hitler and a few of his closest henchmen. Under the overall control of Reichsführer-SS Heinrich Himmler, it had its own secret service, police force, hospitals, radio station, film studios, banks, industries and prisons, which later grew into the infamous concentration camp system. The Waffen-SS was the Nazi Party's private army.

As the SS organization grew, so too did the Waffen-SS. The *Leibstandarte* grew to regimental, or *standarten*, strength, and was employed on security duties at key government buildings and to provide personal protection for senior Nazi leaders. Its raison d'être was to ensure the Nazi regime could not be overthrown by an internal coup. By the late 1930s there was a plethora of Waffen-SS units, including a number of *standarten*, the *Totenkopf* (Death's Head) Division and the motorized *Leibstandarte* Regiment. Following the Nazi invasions of Czechoslovakia (the Sudetenland in October 1938; the rest of the country in March 1939) and Austria (March 1938), Hitler ordered the SS *Deutschland, Germania* and *Der Führer Standarten* to be combined into the SS-Verfügungstruppe (SS-VT) Division. The division was basically a motorized infantry unit with large numbers of motorcycles, halftracks and light artillery. It fought during the Blitzkrieg campaigns against Poland in September 1939 and the Low Countries and France in May 1940. The *Totenkopf* and *Leibstandarte* also took part in these operations, although the former unit committed a number of atrocities.

In late 1940, as Hitler was mustering his forces for Operation Barbarossa – the invasion of the Soviet Union – he ordered a massive expansion of the Waffen-SS. The *Leibstandarte* was up-rated to a full motorized division. The SS-VT was spilt in two to create the *Deutschland* (soon renamed *Das Reich*) and *Wiking* Motorized Divisions. The four Waffen-SS divisions were each some 16,000 men strong and now boasted 150mm howitzers, 75mm antitank guns and the deadly 88mm flak or antiaircraft guns. The only tracked armoured fighting vehicles assigned to them at this point in the war were Sturmgeschütz (StuG) III assault guns armed with short-barrelled 75mm guns.

The Waffen-SS motorized divisions were in the thick of the action during the invasion of Russia in June 1941, with the *Leibstandarte* and *Wiking* Divisions fighting in the south, and the other two divisions leading the German advance in the north and central sectors. By the spring of 1942, the four divisions had suffered horrendous casualties in desperate defensive actions during the Soviet winter counteroffensive of 1941–42, and were barely functioning as fighting formations. They each mustered 2000 men fit for action. However, their tenacity in defence against massive odds, and especially their refusal to yield ground, greatly impressed Hitler.

In the summer and autumn of 1942, as stated above, the *Leibstandarte*, *Das Reich* and *Totenkopf* Divisions were withdrawn from the Eastern Front and moved to France for reorganizing as Waffen-SS panzergrenadier divisions. *Wiking* remained in the southern sector of the Eastern Front and was steadily reinforced with so-called "foreign volunteers" from occupied countries, but it was never as powerful as the three original SS panzergrenadier divisions.

The Waffen-SS panzergrenadier divisions were so lavishly equipped with tanks and armoured vehicles that, in reality, they were more powerful that army line panzer divisions.

The strike power of the Waffen-SS divisions lay in their panzer regiments, which boasted two battalions of tanks. In 1942 a tank battalion had three companies – one of heavy Panzer IVs and two with lighter Panzer IIIs, each having a complement of 22 tanks. The *Leibstandarte*'s companies, however, all had Panzer IVs in frontline roles, with Panzer IIIs reduced to command tasks. For added punch, each Waffen-SS panzer regiment also had a company of the monster Tiger I tanks attached. By mid-1944 these companies had grown into battalions. This organization was constantly evolving, but it is important to realize that once a panzer regiment was committed to battle it was common for less than half of its tanks to be fit for action at any one time.

The 25.4-tonne (25-ton) Panzer IV was the main German frontline tank of the war, and it was progressively up-armoured and up-gunned to meet the challenge of new Allied tanks. In late 1942, the main version in service with the Waffen-SS was the Ausf G model, which boasted a long-barrelled L/48 75mm cannon. With the introduction of this version, the armour balance on the Eastern Front swung back in Germany's favour after the surprise appearance of the Soviet T-34 medium tank the previous autumn. During mid-1943, the Panzer IVs were fitted with so-called armoured "skirts" along the side of the hull and around the turret to deflect Soviet antitank rounds. This later feature often led to the tank being mistakenly identified by the enemy as a Tiger I. Many Panzer IIIs were also equipped with skirt armour in an attempt to keep them battle-worthy, but the tank's 50mm cannon could not knock out a T-34, which was armed with the 76.2mm F-34 gun.

The Tiger I was introduced into Waffen-SS service in late 1942 after making its combat debut with the army in August 1942. At some 57.9 tonnes (57 tons), it was truly a battlefield monster, and armed with the high-velocity 88mm cannon it could knock out a Russian T-34 at a range of almost 2000m

(6560ft). Thanks to its 100mm- (3.93in-) thick front armour, the Tiger I was almost impervious to the 76.2mm cannon fitted to the Russian tanks of this period. In late-1944, the Tiger I was replaced with the truly monster Tiger II, or King Tiger tank.

Contrary to popular myth, the Waffen-SS was not equipped with the famous Panzer V Panther tank until the late summer of 1943, so during the battles around Kharkov and at Kursk, the Waffen-SS had to make do with Panzer IIIs and IVs, backed up by a couple of dozen Tiger Is.

At the heart of the Waffen-SS divisions were their panzergrenadier regiments. These units were able to trace their lineage back to the original SS standarten, and they made great play of their Nazi heritage. They generally had honorific titles as well as numerical designations. For example, *Das Reich* had the *Deutschland* and *Der Führer* Regiments, *Totenkopf* had the Thule (later *Totenkopf*) and *Theodor Eicke* Regiments, and *Wiking* had the Germania, Nordland and Westland Regiments. The *Leibstandarte*, however, was unique in that all its sub-units included numerical designations and the title *Leibstandarte SS Adolf Hitler*, abbreviated to *Wiking*.

During the autumn of 1942, the panzer-grenadier regiments had equipment lavished on them to turn them into self-contained armoured units in their own right. One panzergrenadier battalion in the division received armoured halftracks to allow it to go into action alongside the panzer regiment. The other battalions retained their soft-skinned transport, but also had 120mm mortars, 20mm flak guns, 75mm antitank guns and 150mm Bison light howitzers. These were mostly self-propelled on halftrack chassis. When fully up to strength, a Waffen-SS panzergrenadier regiment boasted some 3200 men in late 1942.

Heavy firepower was provided by the artillery regiment, which received self-propelled 105mm Wespe and 150mm Hummel howitzers, as well as wheeled versions of those guns.

Support elements

Supporting the "teeth regiments" of the division were antitank, reconnaissance, assault gun, antiaircraft, and combat engineer (pioneer) battalions. During late 1942, the Waffen-SS started to receive the StuG III Ausf F, which featured the powerful L/48 75mm cannon, to equip its assault gun battalions. These vehicles packed a powerful punch and had heavy armoured protection, and so were much in demand to support panzergrenadier operations. The antitank companies in the panzergrenadier regiments and the divisional antitank battalion, as well as the reconnaissance battalion, also used the Marder III antitank gun, which utilized an obsolete Czech 38(t) tank chassis and mounted the long-barrelled L/40 75mm or 76.2mm cannon. These bore the brunt of defensive antitank tasks, freeing the panzer regiment to take the lead in offensive action.

There were also strong communications, medical, supply and maintenance elements assigned to each division. Mobile repair teams were a key element because they were able to recover damaged tanks from battlefields and return them to action within days. This ensured the divisions did not have to wait weeks for new tanks to arrive from factories thousands of kilometres from the front. At full strength, a Waffen-SS panzergrenadier division comprised around 21,000 men. The nearest Red Army equivalent was the Tank Corps, which in 1943 boasted some 12,000 men, more than 180 T-34/76 tanks and some 60 SU-76 assault guns or SU-85 tank destroyers.

The SS Panzer Corps headquarters was activated in the summer of 1942 in Germany, before moving to France to oversee the establishment of the Waffen-SS panzergrenadier divisions. The headquarters mustered several thousand specialist staff officers and technical experts. Its core was a radio communications unit to allow the corps commander to talk to his divisions and higher headquarters. There was also a artillery command cell to allow the firepower of all the divisional artillery regiments to be moved around the battlefield in a coordinated manner.

Depending on the battlefield situation, the corps could also take under its command army level artillery units with 210mm towed guns or mobile rocket launchers, known as Nebelwerfers. In 1942 the Waffen-SS did not have any of its own such units, but they were formed by late 1943 to boost its firepower. In the middle of 1943 the first of three Waffen-SS heavy tank battalions was formed, but the battalions were not ready for action until the spring of 1944, when they went into action during the Normandy campaign.

In late 1942 the SS Panzer Corps was the only such formation in existence, but Hitler was keen to expand his private army even further, and so six months later he ordered the establishment of a second corps, to be titled I SS Panzer Corps *Leibstandarte Adolf Hitler*. The original corps headquarters was then retitled II SS Panzer Corps just prior to the Battle of Kursk in July 1943. I SS Panzer Corps was to be made up of the *Leibstandarte* Division and the soon-to-be-formed Hitlerjugend Panzergrenadier Division, although the two divisions did not serve together under the command of the corps headquarters until the summer of 1944, because of the requirement for the *Leibstandarte* in Italy and Russia. Once II SS Panzer Corps was withdrawn from Russia in the autumn of 1943, it was put in command of the *Hohenstaufen* and *Frundsberg* Panzergrenadier Divisions, which had been forming in France since December 1943. In autumn 1943, the final stage in the evolution of the Waffen-SS armoured units occurred when the panzergrenadier divisions began to be renamed panzer divisions and were given numerical designations. For example, the *Leibstandarte* became the 1st SS Panzer Division *Leibstandarte Adolf Hitler*. The renaming was largely a symbolic act, because the Waffen-SS divisions had always been better equipped than most army line panzer divisions for well over a year. For reasons of clarity, this study will refer to them by their honourific titles only.

To understand why the Waffen-SS panzer divisions were so successful in battle, it is essential to have some idea of the background and characters of some of the personalities who built and commanded them. While there was no such thing as a typical Waffen-SS officer, there were a number of distinctive groups.

The senior leadership in the early years were nearly all stalwart cronies of Hitler from his time in Munich during the 1920s. "Sepp" Dietrich and Theodor Eicke were old guard Nazis, who liked to cultivate images of themselves as gruff, no-nonsense soldiers. They loved visiting the frontline trenches and swapping war stories with ordinary SS troopers. This bonhomie was largely a way to cover up for their own inadequacies as commanders and tacticians. Both, however, were sensible enough to leave complex technical problems to more talented subordinates. Others of the old Munich gang who joined the ranks of the SS remained behind in Germany and the occupied territories, supervising the mass murder of enemies of the Reich rather than serving at the front. Dietrich, who formed and led the *Leibstandarte* up to mid-1943, was far from the cuddly grandfather figure that Nazi propaganda liked to portray him as. In 1941, for example, he ordered 4000 Russian prisoners to be executed in retaliation for the death of six captured *Leibstandarte* troopers.

The founder of the *Totenkopf*, Eicke, had a reputation as a sadist. He personally shot the SA leader Ernst Röhm during the "Night of the Long Knives". "Papa" Eicke was the first commandant of Dachau concentration camp, and by 1939 was head of the Reich's whole prison camp network. He invented the Death's Head, or *Totenkopf*, insignia that became synonymous with evil and mass murder between 1939 and 1945.

While the likes of Dietrich and Eicke represented the beer hall Nazi heritage of the Waffen-SS, there was also a growing breed of military technocrats who joined the organization during the late 1930s as a means to further their careers. The most famous of these were Paul Hausser, Wilhelm Bittrich and Felix Steiner. They were all officers of the old school, having served in the Kaiser's army during World War I and then in the post-war Reichswehr.

If anyone was responsible for turning the premier Waffen-SS divisions into an elite armoured fighting force, it was Hausser. He retired from the army in 1932 as a lieutenant-general, but within two years he had joined the SS and had set up the first training depot. He was soon put in charge of all Waffen-SS training, and he made a good job of it. He led the *Das Reich* Division during the invasion of Russia and was rewarded with the job of setting up the SS Panzer Corps in the summer of 1942. He led it through to the end of the Normandy campaign in 1944. Some of the old Munich gang did not like him because of his Prussian officer corps pedigree, but Hitler trusted him implicitly.

Bittrich was of a similar mode, and replaced Hausser as commander of the *Das Reich* Division in October 1941. He was heavily involved in raising the *Hohenstaufen* and *Frundsberg* Divisions, and again replaced Hausser as commander of II SS Panzer Corps in 1944. Steiner formed the *Wiking* Division in 1940 and led it in Russia until May 1943. These men, along with Dietrich, were the most competent Waffen-SS panzer corps commanders thanks to their depth of skill and experience.

Working behind the scenes of the Waffen-SS panzer units was a cadre of ex-army professional staff officers who kept them running at a peak of efficiency. The two most prominent were Rudolf Lehman, who was the chief of staff of the *Leibstandarte* until the summer of 1944, and Fritz Kraemer, who was chief of staff of I SS Panzer Corps for most of its existence. They effectively ran their formations to a standard that would be considered appropriate for equivalent army units.

Many of the regimental and battalion commanders in the Waffen-SS during the 1942–43 period – such as Otto Kumm, Kurt Meyer, Hermann Priess, Joachim Peiper, Theodor Wisch, Fritz Witt and Max Wünsche – would all rise to command panzer divisions later in the war. They could, perhaps, be called swashbuckling characters who rose to the top through success in battle during the Blitzkrieg years. They only knew how to soldier the Waffen-SS way: aggressively, taking risks to achieve victory. They were leaders who would be at the centre of the action, ruthlessly driving their men and never giving up. They kept the hard-pushed Waffen-SS panzer divisions fighting during the last two years of the war, when many others would have given up.

The Waffen-SS did not create its own panzer tactics, but adapted existing army techniques to its own distinctive style of fighting. And the ability of Waffen-SS commanders to quickly form their troops into all-arms kampfgruppen to deal with sudden crises or overcome difficult tactical challenges, combined with panzer tactics, paid dividends. And the tight bonds of friendship between the Waffen-SS officer corps worked to their advantage.

Working in kampfgruppen was the norm for Waffen-SS panzer troops, and no major operation would be undertaken without some sort of regrouping of forces to meet specific objectives. The speed at which Waffen-SS commanders could form and launch kampfgruppen into action was often decisive on the Eastern Front, often completely confounding their rigidly hierarchical Red Army opponents, who required detailed orders from higher command before any operation could be undertaken (on the positive side, deliberate planning reduced the strain on inexperienced junior officers).

Kampfgruppen were usually formed around a battalion-sized unit. For assaults and counterattacks, the main units that were used to form kampfgruppen were the division's two panzer battalions, its halftrack-mounted panzergrenadier battalion and the reconnaissance battalion. In defensive operations, the two panzergrenadier regiments bore the brunt of the fighting, with assault gun and antitank detachments attached to augment their firepower.

Forming a kampfgruppe was a routine event and there were well-established procedures for it. The divisional commander would first set out his tactical plan, setting objectives for his regiments. He would then assign divisional assets from his specialist battalions, or elements of other regiments, to specific regimental commanders. The regimental commander, in turn, would divide up his newly assigned assets between his battalion commanders.

The kampfgruppe commander had full tactical command of all the units and equipment assigned to him for the duration of an operation, and only once the mission was completed would they be returned to their parent units for re-assignment. A kampfgruppe was usually named after its commander, which emphasized his instrumental role in its actions. The commander was responsible for all tactical planning and the issuing of operational orders. This meant Waffen-SS battalion and regimental commanders had to be knowledgeable about the all-arms tactics and the capabilities of tanks, infantry, artillery, engineers and antitank weapons.

While most kampfgruppen were formed as a result of deliberate planning, a number were formed on an ad hoc basis when communications with higher headquarters were lost. Often during sudden enemy breakthroughs, an assortment of units would find themselves cut off. It would then be the job of the senior commander on the ground to take charge and organize the defence.

An important part of any kampfgruppe was a halftrack-borne artillery observation party from the division's artillery regiment. The divisional artillery commander would then assign artillery batteries and ammunition supplies to support specific operations. The allocation of fire support was carried out in much the same way as kampfgruppen were formed, with those units in greatest need getting the lion's share of firepower. Luftwaffe forward air controllers would also regularly be assigned to work with kampfgruppe commanders, directing cannon-armed Junkers Ju

87 Stuka dive-bombers and Henschel Hs 129 ground-attack aircraft to their targets, by radio from their armoured halftracks. Waffen-SS battle tactics were designed to capitalize on the capabilities of its equipment and flexible unit organization. Its attack tactics were an evolution of the successful German stormtrooper tactics developed during the final years of World War I, and then refined in the interwar period.

It was the job of the reconnaissance battalion to find weak spots in the enemy's position and then quickly report back to the division intelligence staff on the best way to approach and attack the opposition. The weakest point in the enemy's frontline would then become the target of the division's main effort, or *schwerpunkt* (literally, centre of gravity; thus point of maximum effort). Surprise was essential, since it required the penetration of the enemy line on a narrow front by superior and fast-moving forces.

A powerful kampfgruppe would then be assembled to lead the attack, with a range of capabilities to allow it to bridge rivers, breach minefields and then smash the enemy's resistance. A kampfgruppe had to be self-contained to allow it to overcome sudden obstacles or surprise enemy counterattacks. Once committed to action, this assault force would receive the bulk of the division's artillery support. If a decisive breakthrough was achieved, then more kampfgruppen would be dispatched to capitalize on the initial success.

If possible, Waffen-SS commanders would choose to mount their breakthrough attacks against thinly held sectors of the enemy front, so their combat power would not be dissipated before the start of the decisive phase of the operation. To ensure the breakthrough was successful with the minimum of losses, the Waffen-SS and army developed the *panzerkeil* (armoured wedge) tactics. The most heavily armoured tanks in the division, usually Tigers, would lead the attack because of their relative invulnerability to enemy antitank rounds. Following behind would be lighter tanks and infantry in halftracks. Riding alongside the infantry would be combat engineers, ready to move forward to clear any minefields, clear obstacles or bridge gaps. The kampfgruppe commander would be located just behind the lead tanks, to coordinate the various combat elements under his command.

"No plan survives contact with the enemy," stated Helmuth von Moltke (1800–1891), Prussian field marshal, and so divisional commanders would be constantly monitoring the progress of an attack on the radio net to see how the operation was developing. They were always looking for opportunities to unhinge the enemy's defences, even if this meant sudden changes of plan to capitalize on surprise events. Here, the kampfgruppe system came into its element again, because units could be quickly switched to those kampfgruppen with the best chance of success. The Waffen-SS always reinforced success, pumping reinforcements into breaches in the enemy lines and then pressing on deep into vulnerable rear areas. This type of fast-moving operation often meant that kampfgruppen might be temporarily out of contact with regimental or divisional headquarters, so Waffen-SS commanders were given great latitude to exploit the situation as best they could.

Contrary to popular belief, Waffen-SS panzer commanders preferred not to attack Soviet positions head-on, but rather tried to find undefended gaps in their positions so they could rapidly move deep behind their lines. It was the job of the reconnaissance battalion to push ahead of the lead kampfgruppe to find routes for it to move forward, avoiding minefields, anti-tank ditches and heavily defended positions.

Strictly regimented Soviet forces were often completely confused and defeated by these tactics. Even very small kampfgruppen could cause damage out of all proportion to their size, because of their ability to dodge and weave their way past enemy defences and strike at key points such as command posts, supply dumps and bridges. With their communications to headquarters severed and their lines of retreat cut, Soviet regiments or even divisions could be rendered ineffective. They would then be trapped in pockets to be liquidated at a later date by follow-up infantry units.

In defensive operations, the Waffen-SS aimed to fight in an equally flexible and mobile way as it did during offensive operations. It was the job of the panzergrenadier regiments to hold ground, but counter-attacks played a key role in defeating Soviet breakthroughs. Aggressive use of artillery was the first line of defence, breaking up enemy concentrations in assembly areas before they moved forward. Once attacks were underway, the rapid calling down of artillery and mortar fire on enemy infantry could cause havoc and heavy casualties. It was the job of the Marder self-propelled antitank guns, StuG IIIs and 88mm flak guns assigned to the panzergrenadier regiments to defeat enemy tank attacks.

Stopping enemy tanks
If the enemy attack was pressed forward, then the panzergrenadiers would be ordered to hold their ground to try to separate the enemy tanks from their supporting infantry.

Usually Soviet tank crews would press on forward deep behind the German frontline, even if their tank-riding infantry had been mortared and machined-gunned as they crossed the panzergrenadiers' trench line. More Marder self-propelled antitank guns, StuGs and 88mm flak guns would now be in a position to block the Red Army tanks as they moved around the division's rear area. Carefully prepared tank killing zones would be created in which the heavy antitank weapons could deal with any threats at long range.

Only as a last resort would the Waffen-SS division commit its panzer regiment in "penny packets" to deal with small numbers of enemy tanks. The panzers, usually teamed with the halftrack battalion, would be held back to counterattack against any enemy penetrations that looked like creating dangerous breakthroughs, or to strike deep into the heart of the enemy's own defences to turn the tables on them.

On 31 December 1942, attempts by the German Army to break through to the trapped Stalingrad garrison had failed, and Hitler turned to the SS Panzer Corps to restore the situation. The *Leibstandarte* and *Das Reich* Divisions were loaded onto almost 500 trains and shipped eastwards from 9 January 1943 onwards. *Totenkopf* (which on its own required 120 trains to ship it to the East) was given an extra month's grace after Eicke persuaded the Führer that he needed more time to lick his division into shape for combat. He also raided the French countryside for cars and trucks to ensure his division had adequate transport.

It took almost a month for I SS Panzer Corps to travel across Nazi-occupied Europe to the Eastern Rampart of the Third Reich. In the snow-covered wastes of the eastern

Ukraine, the veteran Waffen-SS officers steadied their raw troopers as the day approached when they would meet the advancing Red Army. They would not have long to wait.

Chapter 3
KHARKOV

I SS Panzer Corps wins its spurs and saves Army Group South.

On 14 March 1943, German radio interrupted its normal broadcasts with a fanfare from a Horst Wessel song (a Nazi anthem commemorating the death of a stormtrooper during a street battle in the 1920s), and announced that Waffen-SS troops had recaptured the Ukrainian city of Kharkov. The five-day battle to win control of the Soviet Union's fourth-largest city was the culmination of a two-month campaign by the Wehrmacht's Army Group South to turn back the advancing Russians after the destruction of the German Sixth Army at Stalingrad. German radio was right to give the success such prominence. In January, Stalin's armies had been running rampant in the Ukraine, with the Wehrmacht falling back in disarray after the massive defeat suffered by the German Army.

Over 150,000 Germans died on the banks of the Volga and a further 91,000, including their commander, Field Marshal Friedrich Paulus, surrendered despite being ordered to fight to the last man by their Führer, Adolf Hitler. While finishing off the remnants of Paulus' battered army, the Russians extended their offensive to the Ukraine, smashing weak German, Hungarian and Italian armies in their path. By early February 1943, Soviet tanks were pushing towards the River Dnieper. Kharkov was threatened, and Russian spearheads were moving south to cut off German troops retreating from the Caucasus through Rostov.

Stalin's generals, however, underestimated the resilience of the Wehrmacht. Army Group South's commander, Field Marshal Erich von Manstein, concentrated his still-powerful panzer divisions and hit the Russians with a stunning counter-punch, just as they reached the limit of their supply lines. The Soviets found themselves outflanked and outgunned. They still had a lot to learn about armoured warfare.

Soviet forces began the final phase of their offensive on 14 January with a massive attack on the overstretched German, Hungarian and Italian armies dug-in along the River Don. Lieutenant-General F.I. Golikov's Voronezh Front and Lieutenant-General N.F. Vatutin's Southwest Front rolled over the defenders with ease and, within two weeks, had pushed 160km (100 miles) westwards. They were now poised to cross the River Donets, which barred the way to Kharkov and the strategically crucial River Dnieper crossings.

To counter this advance, the Germans rushed reinforcements from all over Europe in a desperate bid to rebuild the Eastern Front. North of Kharkov, the army's elite *Grossdeutschland* Motorized Division, supported by the 88th and 168th Infantry

Divisions, held the Belgorod area. Two divisions of the SS Panzer Corps, which had just arrived from France, were deployed along the Donets blocking the direct route to Kharkov.

Under SS-Obergruppenführer Paul Hausser, I SS Panzer Corps was superbly equipped with new tanks, armoured halftrack personnel carriers, self-propelled artillery and Nebelwerfer multi-barrel rocket launchers. Holding the

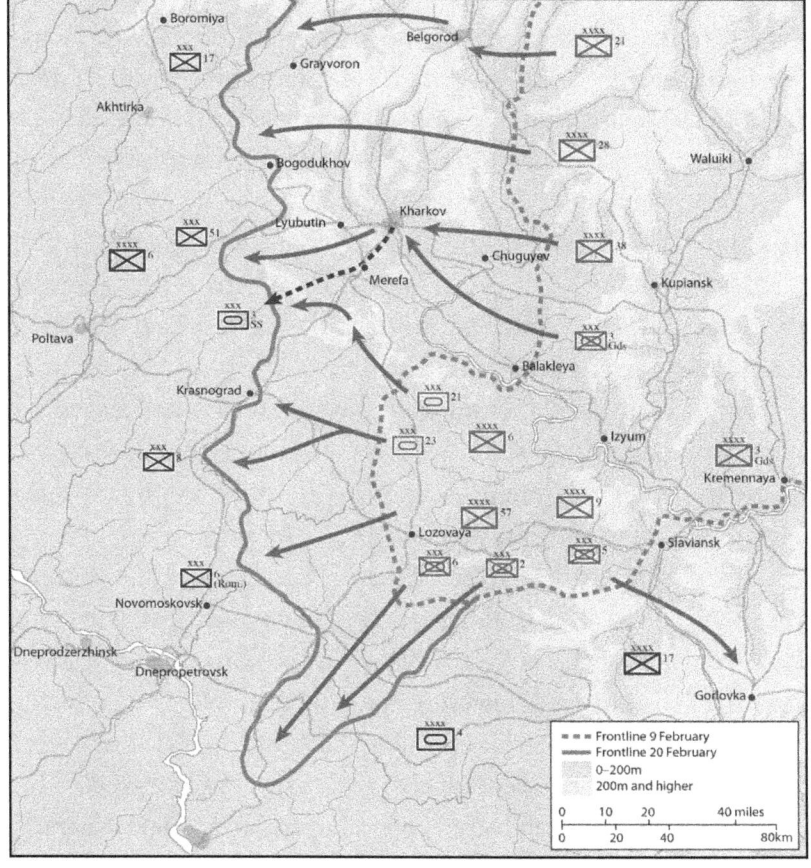

The Second Battle of Kharkov: 9–20 February 1943

Donets line were the *Leibstandarte* and *Das Reich* Divisions. The 1st SS Panzer Regiment of the *Leibstandarte* was the strongest tank unit in the corps, with 52 Panzer IVs, 10 Panzer IIIs and nine Tiger Is. *Das Reich*'s 2nd SS Panzer Regiment had 81 Panzer IIIs and only 21 Panzer IVs, backed up by 10 Tiger Is.

A long journey
The journey from France took almost two weeks, and many of the 200 trains carrying the division were re-routed to avoid Royal Air Force (RAF) bombing and Soviet partisan attacks. These disruptions meant that the divisions arrived at the railhead in Kharkov in dribs and drabs. The first elements to arrive were from the *Leibstandarte*'s 1st Panzergrenadier Regiment, which threw an improvised defensive ring around Kharkov along the frozen banks of the River Donets. Next off the trains on 29 January were the armoured cars and motorcycles of the *Leibstandarte*'s reconnaissance battalion, and they were dispatched to set up a covering screen 80km (50 miles) to the east, to give early warning of any approaching Russians. At the same time the *Deutschland* Panzergrenadier Regiment, of the *Das Reich* Division, was also sent to extend the screen northwards.

As the Waffen-SS troops fanned out across the winter wasteland, they had a series of vicious encounters with the advance guard of the Soviet XVIII Guards Corps. Intermingled with the Russian troops were retreating columns of the hard-pressed German 298th and 320th Infantry Divisions, who had marched across the steppe to seek safety in the west. The German infantry columns were shepherded back towards Kharkov. In a couple of cases, the Waffen-SS reconnaissance troops mounted raids to rescue recently captured infantrymen, racing into Soviet positions on their motorcycles and raking them with machine-gun fire.

The reconnaissance screen fell back deliberately towards Kharkov, and by 4 February 1943 I SS Panzer Corps was almost fully deployed in its main defensive position along the Donets. South of Kharkov there was a void of 160km (100 miles) between the Waffen-SS corps and the left flank of the First Panzer Army. Manstein was moving up units of the Fourth Panzer Army to fill the gap, but they would take time to arrive, leaving Kharkov very exposed to encirclement by Golikov's tanks in the interim.

Hausser's Waffen-SS troops held their front along the Donets with grim determination against furious attacks by the Soviet XII and XV Tank Corps (a Soviet tank corps was equivalent in tank strength to a German panzer division) from Lieutenant-General P.S. Rybalko's Third Tank Army until 10 February (each tank army had two tank corps, a separate tank brigade and support units). This brave stand only played into the Soviets' hands. Russian troops were pushing around the flanks of Hausser's corps and there was a real prospect of Stalingrad being repeated, albeit on a much smaller scale. Major-General K.S. Moskalenko's Fortieth Army, with IV Tank Corps in the lead, turfed the *Grossdeutschland* Division out of Belgorod and sent it heading south to Kharkov.

In their positions east of the city, the Waffen-SS divisions inflicted heavy casualties against Soviet human-wave attacks. Hausser, now dubbed "Papa" by his men, took great delight in visiting the frontline to watch the action. He was reportedly particularly impressed by the performance of the new MG 42 belt-fed machine gun, which was used in action by the Waffen-SS for the first time by the *Leibstandarte*'s 1st Panzergrenadier

Regiment on 4 February. Hundreds of dead Russians were later found piled in front of the Waffen-SS position.

This was a see-saw battle, with daily Soviet probing attacks and regular German counterattacks. The brunt of these assaults were borne by the Waffen-SS panzergrenadiers, backed up by small assault gun detachments. Paul Hausser was keeping his panzer regiments well behind the frontline, ready to deal with any major enemy penetration of his front.

To the south of the Waffen-SS, Vatutin took advantage of the lack of opposition in front of him to push his troops tirelessly forward. The Sixth Army, with two tank corps, two infantry corps and a cavalry corps raced for the Dnieper crossing at Dnepropetrovsk, while Lieutenant-General M.M. Popov's Front Mobile Group of four tank corps pushed south, aiming for Krasnoarmeiskoye and the Sea of Azov.

Overestimating the capabilities of his prized Waffen-SS troops, Hitler ordered them to attack southeastwards to close the gap with the First Panzer Army. Two groups were formed for the operation. A strong covering force was to remain around Kharkov under command of *Das Reich*, which also included the *Leibstandarte*'s 2nd Panzergrenadier Regiment and elements of the division's Tiger tank company, artillery and flak regiments. Hausser's corps headquarters and the *Grossdeutschland* Division also remained in the city, along with the 298th Infantry Division.

The covering force fought an increasingly desperate defensive battle, and the frontline had to be pulled back to free troops for the coming operation to the south of the city. By 12 February, the Soviet VI Guards Cavalry Corps had punched a hole in the line separating the *Leibstandarte* from the 320th Infantry Division. Surrounded and burdened with thousands of wounded men, the army division needed help fast. A kampfgruppe was formed under SS-Sturmbannführer Joachim Peiper, then commander of the 2nd Panzergrenadier Regiment's armoured personnel carrier battalion, to rescue the division. He was given a column of ambulances and a detachment of StuG III assault guns for the mission. The kampfgruppe punched through the Russian front after destroying several tanks, and pushed 48km (30 miles) behind enemy lines to find the beleaguered infantry division. After loading up the ambulances, Peiper's men headed back to German lines, but a Soviet ski battalion had moved into place to block their path and destroy the main bridge over the River Udy, which the Waffen-SS column had to cross to return to Kharkov. The Waffen-SS kampfgruppe attacked and cleared out the Russians in house-to-house fighting, before repairing the bridge for the ambulances.

However, the hastily repaired structure could not take the heavy weight of the Waffen-SS assault guns and armoured halftracks, so Peiper ordered his men back behind Russian lines to find a more suitable crossing. They returned to the *Leibstandarte*'s lines after suffering only a handful of casualties and rescuing the 320th Infantry Division, which was soon able to return to frontline duty after being fed and housed by the Waffen-SS supply units. This was only a temporary respite for Hausser, though. To the north of Kharkov, the *Grossdeutschland* Division was being pushed back into the northern outskirts of the city. No forces could be spared to counter this dangerous pincer because of Hitler's insistence that I SS Panzer Corps' attack group continue with its southward push from Merefa. This would involve the commitment of the *Leibstandarte*'s powerful panzer regiment for the first time.

The large attack group, under the *Leibstandarte*'s commander, SS-Obergruppenführer Josef "Sepp" Dietrich, was ordered to lead the attack forward on 11 February. Pushing directly southwards into the flank of the Soviet VI Guards Cavalry Corps was the *Leibstandarte*'s 1st Panzergrenadier Regiment with its lorry-borne infantry, and the 2nd Battalion of the division's panzer regiment. *Das Reich*'s *Der Führer* Panzergrenadier Regiment reinforced this effort, while SS-Obersturmbannführer Kurt "Panzer" Meyer led the *Leibstandarte*'s reconnaissance battalion deployed on the right to seal the Russian incursion with a large flanking move. He was given a full panzer battalion to support this daring move.

Heavy snow drifts slowed the advance and made it impossible for the Waffen-SS panzers to take the lead in the attack for the first few hours. Stuka dive-bombers strafed Russian columns, and the Waffen-SS units made good progress, clearing the enemy from village after village. By early evening Meyer and his men had all but completed their encircling move, while the main attack columns surprised and destroyed a number of Russian formations. On 12 February, Meyer's advance continued under the cover of a massive snowstorm. Russian and German tank columns became intermingled in the poor visibility conditions, but the Waffen-SS column pressed on regardless. The following day, Meyer's kampfgruppe found itself cut off in Bereka, which blocked the Soviet line of retreat from the pocket created by the Waffen-SS operation. During the night, six tanks of the *Leibstandarte*'s Panzer Regiment, under Max Wünsche, broke through the Soviet ring to reinforce Meyer, and he then used the tanks to sweep the neighbourhood of Soviet infantry. For the next two days the attack group tightened the grip on the trapped Russian cavalry corps, and swept village after village for stragglers. *Leibstandarte* panzers led these attacks, neutralizing isolated Russian tanks so the panzergrenadiers could move forward in their armoured halftracks. By the time the Waffen-SS had finished its work, the 7000 Soviet soldiers of VI Guards Cavalry Corps had been scattered, 10 of its 16 tanks destroyed, 3000 troops wounded and a further 400 captured. Other Russian troops were moving forward to help their comrades, however, and soon the Waffen-SS attack group found itself under attack on three fronts. It was now time for the attack group to fall back.

The main Soviet force dodged Hausser's punch, slipping in behind the advancing Waffen-SS men to try to cut them off from Kharkov and split up the already fragmented German front even more. These were desperate days for the Waffen-SS panzer troops. With temperatures dropping to minus 40 degrees centigrade, it was vital to hold towns or villages to provide vital shelter from the elements. Retreat into the freezing night spelt disaster, so the Waffen-SS grenadiers were literally fighting for their own survival.

In these see-saw battles the superior equipment, training and determination of the Waffen-SS tank crews usually meant they came out on top, but their panzer kampfgruppen could not be everywhere, and by 14 February Kharkov was virtually surrounded. To compound the problem, an uprising had broken out in the city and Hausser feared that his corps headquarters units, *Das Reich* and *Grossdeutschland* would share the same fate as Paulus at Stalingrad. He wanted to order an evacuation through a narrow corridor to the southwest. Repeated orders from Hitler to hold the city to the last man and bullet were treated with the contempt they deserved. Confusion reigned in the German High Command in the Ukraine, with no one wanting to be seen to disobey the Führer's direct orders. In the end, though, Hausser issued the orders to pull out on 15 February. By the time Hitler found out and had issued countermanding orders, the *Das Reich* Division was on its way to safety and there was no going back. The *Das Reich* and *Leibstandarte* panzergrenadiers set up an improvised defence line to the south of Kharkov, but Soviet tanks were close on their heels, inflicting a steady stream of casualties before the Waffen-SS units could break clear.

With I SS Panzer Corps safely out of Kharkov, Manstein was able to complete the reorganization of his panzer divisions for their counterstroke. An unannounced visit by Hitler, furious at the loss of Kharkov, to Manstein's headquarters at Zaporozhe on 17 February interrupted the field marshal's preparations. Hitler had intended to dismiss Manstein for the loss of the city and order an immediate northwards attack by I SS Panzer Corps to retake Kharkov. Fortunately for the field marshal, the sound of Russian artillery near his command post brought the Führer to his senses and he left in a hurry, to allow Manstein to get on with sorting out the Soviets. Manstein was also helped by the fact that the Waffen-SS *Totenkopf* Division got stuck in mud after a sudden thaw during the day, making it unavailable for Hitler's proposed attack.

Manstein's plan called for two Waffen-SS divisions to strike southwest from Krasnograd into the western flank of the Soviet Sixth Army, while the Fourth Panzer Army drove northwards to push the remaining elements of the western Soviet attack force onto the guns of the Waffen-SS panzers. Farther east, the First Panzer Army would take the offensive against Popov's Front Mobile Group and complete the destruction of the Soviet forces west of the River Donets.

The Russians proved easy meat for the panzers. After two months of continuous fighting, Popov's group was down to 50 worn-out tanks and 13,000 men fit for battle. Lieutenant-General F.M. Khatritonov's Sixth Army was in an equally perilous state, with many of its 150 tanks stranded through lack of fuel. Of most help to Manstein, however, were orders from Vatutin (who was still convinced the Germans were retreating) for the Soviet troops to keep advancing.

As this battle was developing, Hausser set about reorganizing his corps for offensive action. The *Leibstandarte* was to be the anvil of the offensive based around Krasnograd, while *Das Reich* and the newly arrived *Totenkopf* Division swung south and then northwards, forcing the Russians back onto the guns of the *Leibstandarte*. The arrival of the *Totenkopf* at Krasnograd on the morning of 19 February, with its 81 Panzer IIIs, 22 Panzer IVs, and nine Tiger Is, completed I SS Panzer Corps' order of battle for perhaps its most famous victory. In the afternoon Manstein ordered the attack to proceed.

A 96km (60-mile) road march brought *Das Reich* and *Totenkopf* to their jump-off positions at Novomoskovsk on 20 February. Pushing westwards, they sliced through the immobilized XXV Tank Corps and IV Guards and XV Guards Rifle Corps near Pavlograd. These units were in bad shape after Luftwaffe antitank aircraft caught the Russian armour by surprise earlier in the morning. XXXXVIII Panzer Corps was already attacking from the south, so the Waffen-SS attack sliced into the side of the already-stalled Russian columns. *Totenkopf* was assigned the northern axis of the attack, and *Das Reich* pushed farther south and then turned eastwards to Pavlograd, before swinging northwards. The

Waffen-SS men raced forward at such a break-neck speed that Soviet and German troops often became intermingled. A panzer kampfgruppe of *Das Reich* spearheading the division's advance seized a key bridge outside Pavlograd on 22 February. Two *Das Reich* Panzer IIIs and a Tiger held the bridge for several hours, destroying three T-34s that tried to take the bridge back.

The two Waffen-SS divisions trapped the Soviet I Guards Tank Corps and two rifle divisions. The Waffen-SS Tigers and Panzer IVs knocked out the Russian tanks and antitank guns with ease at long range with their powerful 88mm and 75mm cannons, before panzergrenadiers closed in to mop-up pockets of isolated Soviet infantry who offered resistance in the snow-bound villages. Elements of Soviets divisions were smashed in the attack, with most of the men just abandoning their tanks and vehicles and fleeing into the surrounding forests. For five days the two Waffen-SS divisions meandered through huge columns of abandoned and destroyed vehicles, machine-gunning small groups of Russian soldiers hiding amid the carnage. The Soviet Sixth Army had ceased to exist.

The death of Theodor Eicke

The Soviets exacted a heavy price on the *Totenkopf* Division for its victory, however. The division's commander, SS-Obergruppenführer Theodor Eicke, flew forward in his Fieseler Storch light aircraft to visit his spearhead units on 26 February. The infamous SS general ordered his pilot to land near a village that he believed was occupied by *Totenkopf* troops. In fact, the men on the ground were a group of cut-off Russian soldiers, and Eicke's aircraft was ripped apart in mid-air by antiaircraft artillery fire as it approached the ground. The following day Waffen-SS troops cleared the village and recovered the mutilated body of the former concentration camp commander.

From the north, the *Leibstandarte* Division was conducting an aggressive defence of its line in the snow, aimed at neutralizing the advance elements of the Soviet Third Tank Army. *Leibstandarte* kampfgruppen were launched forward on a daily basis to destroy large Soviet formations spotted by Luftwaffe aerial reconnaissance. The Waffen-SS men infiltrated at night through the thinly held Soviet front to ambush the enemy. Bursting from forests, the kampfgruppen usually took the Russians by surprise, and within minutes their panzers and armoured halftracks would be right in the middle of the enemy positions, spreading mayhem and destruction. Their job complete, the Germans would then pull back to regroup and rearm for the next foray.

On 17 February the *Leibstandarte*'s reconnaissance battalion, reinforced with panzers, wiped out a Soviet infantry regiment in the first big raid. Three days later Peiper's armoured infantry battalion cleared out 750 Russians, three tanks and dozens of antitank guns from a heavily defended village during a night attack.

SS-Obersturmbannführer Kurt "Panzer" Meyer was given command of a kampfgruppe of panzers and reconnaissance troops on 19 February, with the mission of destroying a large enemy forcing advancing westwards. His panzer company destroyed a Russian battalion in the afternoon.

At dawn on 21 February, his column had taken up ambush positions near the town of Jerememkevka. Meyer spotted a long column of Soviet troops moving across the snow-covered steppe, totally unaware of the imminent danger. The attack began with a daredevil charge into the middle of the column by a reconnaissance team in VW Schwimmwagen amphibious jeeps, led by Meyer himself. One vehicle was blown up by a mine, but within minutes the others were among the stunned Russians, raking them with machine-gun fire. Panzer IV tanks then burst out of the woods at the head and tail of the column, cutting off any hope of retreat. Several hundred Russians were slaughtered and a dozen artillery pieces captured. The following night Meyer's force launched another raid on an unsuspecting Russian column, with similar results. The fighting on the northern sector of the division's front was also intense, with the panzer regiment having to be sent to relieve its pioneer battalion, which had been surrounded by a surprise Soviet attack.

On 23 February Meyer's battle group was ordered forward, again ambushing a Soviet divisional headquarters and a whole divisional artillery group. A surprise panzer attack charged into a Russian-held town, and within five hours the *Leibstandarte* men had killed 1000 enemy soldiers and captured 30 heavy artillery pieces.

While the *Leibstandarte*, *Das Reich* and *Totenkopf* Divisions were striking back at the Soviet spearheads south of Kharkov, on the right flank of the German front the *Wiking* Panzergrenadier Division was involved in a series of brutal skirmishes to hold back the enemy advance. A powerful Soviet tank force, led by III and IV Tank Corps and supported by hundreds of ski troops, was pushing south into the breach in the German line, just to the west of the First Panzer Army. Manstein hoped to seal the gap in the front from the west with I SS Panzer Corps, and from the east with the armoured units of the Fourth Panzer Army being brought up from the Caucasus.

By 8 February, the Soviets had taken the key rail junctions at Krasnoarmeiskoye and Gishino, in a surprise push 80km (50 miles) behind the left flank of the First Panzer Army. First on the scene to counter this dangerous incursion was the *Wiking* Division, closely followed by the 7th and 11th Panzer Divisions. These were not fresh and superbly equipped divisions. They had been in action continuously for almost three months, and were down to only 2000 fighting troops each. *Wiking* alone could not muster more than five battered old Panzer III tanks fit for action. The Waffen-SS men could barely stabilize the front, let alone press forward to clear out the incursion. Only his strong artillery regiment enabled the *Wiking*'s commander, SS-Obergruppenführer Felix Steiner, to contain the Russian tanks.

On 12 February, the *Wiking* Division launched an outflanking attack into the eastern edge of Krasnoarmeiskoye itself and northwards to Gishino, but it broke down in the face of fanatical Soviet resistance. For the next week, the Waffen-SS men and an army infantry division fought vicious street battles to contain the Soviet forces from breaking out of the town. X Soviet Tank Corps arrived to support the advance from Krasnoarmeiskoye, but the Soviet troops in the region were also very weak by this time, with no more than two dozen tanks available to fight the Waffen-SS troops.

The 7th Panzer Division was now thrown into the battle, attacking into the east of the city, while the *Wiking* Division tried to storm in from the west. Luftwaffe Stukas supported the assault, but the Russians held firm. XXXX Panzer Corps now ordered the *Wiking* and the 7th Panzer Divisions to bypass Krasnoarmeiskoye. In a Blitzkrieg-style advance they were to defeat the Soviets in a battle of manoeuvre. The attack opened on 19 February with a sweep north from Krasnoarmeiskoye across the open steppe, trapping several thousand Russians and 12 tanks. A large Soviet force broke out two days later. Now the remaining elements of the Popov Mobile Group turned tail and headed north as fast as possible.

The rearguard of X Tank Corps, with 16 T-34s, tried to halt the *Wiking* Division on 21 February. Again the *Wiking* swept around the Soviet defences and rolled northwards. This was a no-holds-barred pursuit. The handful of Waffen-SS tanks of the division's only panzer battalion were leading the way, supported by armoured cars and motorcycle troops. Every couple of kilometres, the advance guard would run into the remains of a Soviet vehicle column, either abandoned because of lack of fuel or devastated by Luftwaffe air strikes. The Waffen-SS men did not stop to investigate but pressed on. They did not outnumber the enemy, so victory would only come by moving faster than the Soviets, and keeping enemy commanders confused as to where the Germans would strike next.

The *Wiking*, 7th and 11th Panzer Divisions caught up with the remains of four Soviet infantry divisions and four tank corps at Barvenkovo on 25 February. More than 50 T-34s were dug in to the south of the town, but they had run out of fuel so were powerless to manoeuvre against the rampaging panzers. In a three-day battle, the 11th Panzer Division attacked directly from the south, while the *Wiking* and 7th Panzer Divisions swept around the Russians' flanks. The Soviets, however, kept open a corridor to the Donets at Izyum, and most of their troops managed to escape the pincers – but all of their tanks had to be left behind.

By the end of the February the first phase of Manstein's offensive was complete. The Russian thrust to the south had been defeated and the gap in the German front closed by the dramatic intervention of I SS Panzer Corps. The German High Command claimed 615 enemy tanks, 354 artillery pieces, 69 antiaircraft guns destroyed, 23,000 Russians dead and 9000 prisoners, during the first phase of the counterattack. Manstein now turned his attention to the large Soviet armoured force guarding the southern approach to Kharkov. In an ill-considered move to blunt the German drive, Rybalko's Third Tank Army swung south to take on I SS Panzer Corps. In a matter of days his army would be cut to pieces.

The attack got underway on 24 February, with heavy tank attacks against the northern flank of the *Leibstandarte* Division. The frontline panzergrenadier units had to call up panzer support to drive off the Soviet 11th Cavalry Division, for the loss of five tanks and 500 dead. A panzer attack on the following day surprised a Soviet artillery regiment and destroyed more than 50 howitzers. An attack force of 30 German tanks used a valley to advance behind the Russian artillery, and when they broke cover the Soviets fled. Soviet pressure on the *Leibstandarte* Division continued on 26 February, with a heavy tank attack by T-34 medium and KV-1 heavy tanks. A total of 12 vehicles were destroyed by Waffen-SS antitank teams.

The Soviets now pushed their last tank reserves southwards in a bid to drive a wedge between the *Leibstandarte* and its sister divisions, which were moving northwards after they had finished clearing up what was left of the Soviet Sixth Army. Hausser ordered the *Leibstandarte* to pull back on 28 February to entice the Russians to move farther south into a trap. Three days later, I SS Panzer Corps was advancing again. The Luftwaffe caught the Russian tanks in the open and broke up their attack formations.

The *Leibstandarte*'s panzers then moved eastwards, destroying nine tanks and 15 antitank guns. A link-up with the *Der Führer*

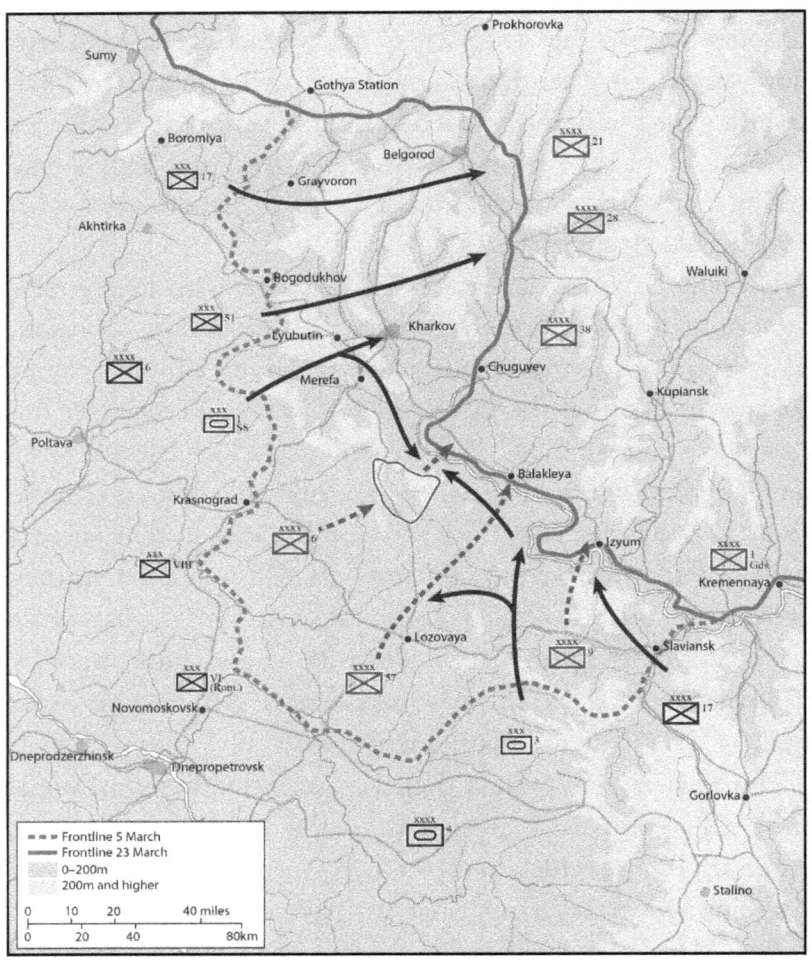

The Third Battle of Kharkov: 5–23 March 1943

Panzergrenadier Regiment, of the *Das Reich* Division, was made on 3 March. Meyer's reconnaissance battalion achieved another link-up with *Totenkopf* later in the day, to complete the ring around a huge pocket of Soviet troops. For two days infantry elements of I SS Panzer Corps cleared up the pocket, but there were not enough troops and so thousands of Russians escaped. In the *Leibstandarte*'s section of the pocket, prisoners from four Russian infantry divisions and a tank brigade were picked up. VI Guards Cavalry Corps managed to escape the trap, but large parts of IV, XXII and XV Tank Corps were destroyed. A further 61 Soviet tanks, 225 guns, 60 motor vehicles and 9000 dead were left on the icy battlefield.

Rybalko's defeat left Kharkov wide open, and Manstein soon set his panzers rolling north again to capture the prize. He planned to push I SS Panzer Corps forward to bypass Kharkov from the west, and then swing east around the top of the city to the Donets and block the escape route of its defenders, as XXXXVIII Panzer Corps assaulted the city from the south. To complete the victory, the reinforced *Grossdeutschland* Division, which had recently received a new tank detachment of 42 Panzer IVs and nine Tigers, would strike north to Belgorod to block any interference with the attack on Kharkov. It was to be supported by the *Totenkopf*'s reconnaissance battalion during this phase of the operation. Only the imminent arrival of the spring thaw could save Kharkov from the Germans.

Closing the trap

Hausser pulled his panzer corps into an attack formation: *Totenkopf* on the left; *Leibstandarte* in the centre; and *Das Reich* on the right. Rocket launchers were positioned to support the attack, and Tiger I tanks moved forward to spearhead the assault operation.

According to plan, the first attack went in on 6 March and, four days later, the Waffen-SS panzers had reached a line level with Kharkov. To the east, the army panzer divisions were held up for five days by a determined stand by the 25th and 62nd Guards Rifle Divisions.

Heavy air strikes preceded the Waffen-SS advance, with *Das Reich* receiving priority support. The Soviet defences were weak and disorganized, so the German advanced pushed all before it. Again, the *Leibstandarte*'s reconnaissance battalion was teamed with a strong panzer detachment to spearhead the division's advance. This time Meyer had the use of Tiger I tanks for the first time. South of the town of Valki, Meyer's kampfgruppe was confronted by a 'pak-front', or network of 56 76.2mm anti-tank guns. With panzergrenadiers sheltering behind the turrets of the tanks, Meyer ordered his panzers to charge forward. Their speed meant Waffen-SS men overran the antitank guns easily, but two dozen T-34 tanks lay in wait ahead, hidden in a village. The Panzer IVs started to take casualties before a Tiger was called up. The lead Tiger got to within 100m (328ft) of the village when a T-34 opened fire. It hit the Tiger on the turret, but the Soviet 76mm shell barely scratched the German tank's paint. The Tiger blasted the T-34 with its 88mm gun, blowing off the turret and taking half of a nearby house with it. During the next hour the Tigers cleared out a dozen T-34s and the rest fled at high speed. The rest of the kampfgruppe was, meanwhile, clearing out the remaining Soviet infantry and gun crews who had hidden in the village as the tank duel ragged in its streets.

The following day Meyer's men were again confronted by a pak-front on the outskirts of Valki. A tank attack was ordered, but several panzers were lost to enemy fire before they overran the gun pits. German tanks literally crushed the antitank guns under their tracks when the Soviet gunners refused to flee.

Das Reich's Der Führer Panzergrenadier Regiment led the division's attack, and it was soon within striking distance of the western outskirts of Kharkov. The Totenkopf Division was not making as good progress out on the left wing because of heavy resistance from VI Guards Cavalry Corps. The Totenkopf's reconnaissance battalion was also fighting with the Grossdeutschland Division's left-flank units and was unable to help out, after getting bogged down for several days in a battle with three Soviet infantry divisions.

At this point, Nazi politics and pride entered the tactical equation and threw a massive spanner in the works of Manstein's counteroffensive. Stung by his ungraceful departure from Kharkov three weeks earlier, Hausser was determined not to allow the army to share in the glory of recapturing his prize. In direct disobedience of orders to keep his tanks out of the city, Hausser planned to send the Das Reich Division into Kharkov from the west, while the Leibstandarte Division pushed in from the north. The Totenkopf Division was to continue its original mission to encircle the city.

For five days the Waffen-SS men battled through fanatical resistance in the concrete high-rise housing blocks that dominated the approaches to the city centre. The remnants of the Soviet Third Tank Army, reinforced by armed citizens, fought for every street and building.

By 10 March the Totenkopf and Leibstandarte had cleared the town of Dergachi, 16km (10 miles) to the north of Kharkov, of Soviet defenders, opening the way for the Leibstandarte to swing southwards down two main roads into the heart of the city. Two large kampfgruppen were formed, based around each of the division's panzergrenadier regiments, for the assault operation and they were reinforced with strong assault gun, 88mm flak gun and Nebelwefer rocket launcher support. A third kampfgruppe made up of the reconnaissance battalion and a panzer battalion, led by Meyer, was to push farther eastwards and then enter Kharkov to close the escape route of the defenders. This took him through a heavily wooded and swampy region, which required plenty of guile and cunning to safely navigate. The column got hopelessly disorganized in the woods, as the tanks were pressed into service to drag bogged-down reconnaissance jeeps out of the soft mud created as a consequence of an early thaw. Meyer, of course, was at the head of the column and, as he emerged from the forest, he saw a large Soviet infantry regiment blocking his path. Fortunately, a roving Stuka patrol intervened and devastated the Russian column.

The Soviets rushed reinforcements, including a tank brigade and an elite brigade of NKVD security troops, into the city to try to set up an improvised defence line. Hausser was determined not to let the Russians build up their strength, so the *Leibstandarte* and *Das Reich* Divisions were ordered to press on with a night assault during the early hours of 11 March. The two main *Leibstandarte* assaults immediately ran into heavy resistance, backed by tank counterattacks all along the northern edge of the city. Assault guns were brought up to deal with the enemy tanks, but a vicious duel developed during the day with many Waffen-SS vehicles being put out of action. Progress could only be made with the support of the Nebelwerfer rocket launchers, but even then no breakthrough was achieved.

The key attack, as always, was led by Meyer. With his small column of motorcycles, jeeps, halftracks, two Marder self-propelled antitank guns and nine tanks, he set off in darkness to raid the city. His kampfgruppe weaved its way past a number of Soviet positions, until a pair of T-34s spotted it and opened fire, destroying a panzer. In the confusion, a Soviet antitank crew opened fire and destroyed their own tanks, inadvertently clearing the way for Meyer. He then pressed his column on into the city and it had reached the cemetery by midday, but then had to halt when its tanks ran out of fuel. It then formed an all-round defensive position and waited for relief. Meyer's force was besieged in the cemetery overnight by thousands of Russian troops and armed civilians. The Germans furiously dug in to escape the effects of mortar and artillery fire that was raking their positions.

Hausser now received orders instructing him to call off the attack by *Das Reich*'s *Der Führer* Regiment, but the Waffen-SS commander ignored them. The battle continued to rage in the city throughout the night. To the west, the *Leibstandarte*'s two panzergrenadier regiments began their advance again, this time supported by panzers and 88mm flak guns in the front-assault echelons. Snipers positioned in high-rise flats were blasted with quad 20mm flak cannon mounted on halftracks, while the panzers and flak guns defeated Soviet counterattacks by roving groups of T-34s.

The *Leibstandarte*'s Tigers spearheaded the attacks, each acting as a kind of mobile pillbox. The armoured monsters could park on street corners and easily dominate whole city blocks, while being impervious to enemy fire of all types. Later in the day, Joachim Peiper's armoured personnel carrier battalion was at last able to break through the Red defence to establish a tenuous link with the impetuous Meyer trapped in the cemetery. It brought in much-needed ammunition and fuel before evacuating the wounded. Meyer's depleted kampfgruppe had to remain in position to block any moves by the Russians to reinforce their defences in the centre of the city.

During the night and into the next day, several Waffen-SS kampfgruppen swept through central Kharkov. Every block had to be cleared of snipers, dug-in antitank guns and lone T-34 tanks. The *Leibstandarte* commanders drove their men forward into attack after attack to prevent the Soviets reorganizing their defence. The *Der Führer* Regiment continued to press in from the west to add to the pressure on the Russians in the tractor factory area in eastern Kharkov. The bulk of the *Das Reich* Division was pushing south of the city to cut through large Soviet defensive positions and complete the German ring around the city. *Das Reich*'s tanks cleared a key hill to the southeast of Kharkov on 14 March, destroying 29 antitank guns and scores of bunkers, to break the back of Soviet resistance.

Within the city, the Soviet defenders were still putting up a tenacious resistance. They quickly withdrew from threatened areas, and then used the sewers and ruins to move in behind the Waffen-SS troops. Peiper's armoured halftrack battalion proved invaluable because of its relative invulnerability to rifle fire from the scores of Soviet snipers who were still at large in areas "cleared" by the *Leibstandarte*. Resistance from the population was intense, and thousands of Kharkov's citizens joined in the battle to prevent their city becoming part of the Third Reich again.

The brutal nature of the fighting in Kharkov was emphasized by the fact that more than 1000 Waffen-SS men were killed or wounded. On 14 March the operation to seize the city was complete, and German radio began issuing gloating bulletins about the Soviet defeat. At the Führer's headquarters in East Prussia, plans were being made for a bumper issue of medals to the "heroes" of I SS Panzer Corps.

The main group of Soviet forces in the city was now pulling back southwards into the face of the advancing XXXXVIII Panzer Corps. There was now the possibility of the Germans catching elements of more than 10 enemy divisions and tank corps in a pocket.

On 13 March the *Totenkopf* Division completed its wide sweep north of Kharkov, with SS-Obersturmbannführer Otto Baum's panzergrenadier regiment, backed by a panzer battalion, capturing the Donets crossing at Chuguyev to seal the noose around Rybalko and his men. The *Totenkopf* attack punched south and eastwards to link up with the 6th Panzer Division advancing northeastwards. The *Das Reich*, *Totenkopf*, 6th Panzer and 11th Panzer Divisions then proceeded to chop-up the huge Soviet force hiding in the pocket south of Kharkov. Stalin gave Rybalko permission to give up the defence of the city and break out to the east. The trapped Russians made desperate efforts to escape, staging massive human-wave assaults to break past the *Totenkopf*'s blocking positions along the Donets.

The German noose was not pulled tight enough, and five days later the remnants of the Third Tank Army completed their break-out past Chuguyev, which was then held by weak army panzer divisions. Unlike Hitler, Stalin realized the importance of getting skilled troops out of pockets rather than leaving them to their fate (Rybalko survived the ordeal and went on to command his army with distinction at Kursk during the summer). The exposed *Totenkopf* Division would have been in real trouble if the Soviets had tried to break through to the forces trapped near Kharkov with their reserve Guards tank corps, but it was held back to secure the north Donets line.

To complete the German victory, Hausser dashed panzer kampfgruppen north to link up with the *Grossdeutschland* Division, which had been taking on Soviet armoured units defending Belgorod. An unofficial "race" developed between the *Leibstandarte* and the elite army division for the honour of seizing the last major centre of Soviet resistance in the Ukraine.

The first line of Soviet resistance, some 16km (10 miles) north of Kharkov, was rolled over on 16 March by the *Leibstandarte*'s 2nd Panzergrenadier Regiment, supported by a huge barrage of Nebelwerfer and artillery fire, as well as wave after wave of Stuka dive-bombers. A line of Soviet antitank guns and infantry bunkers ceased to exist. Next day, Peiper's kampfgruppe was unleashed northwards with strong armoured support, including the *Leibstandarte*'s Tiger detachment. This powerful force made easy meat of another enemy antitank gun position during the afternoon.

After a pause during the night to rearm and organize air support, Peiper was off again. On cue, more Stukas attacked a large road-block just after dawn on the morning of 18 March. With the road now clear, Peiper ordered his armoured force forward again. He did not stop until his tanks and armoured carriers were in the centre of Belgorod at 11.35 hours. Eight T-34s encountered on the drive north were destroyed by the Tigers – all other Soviet positions had been ignored. "Sepp" Dietrich flew north in his Storch aircraft to congratulate Peiper on his success. The German *coup de main* operation may have taken the Russians by surprise, but during the afternoon they pulled themselves together and launched a string of armoured counterattacks. The *Leibstandarte*'s panzers repulsed all the attacks, destroying 14 tanks, 38 trucks and 16 antitank guns.

It was not until later in the afternoon, however, when the *Das Reich*'s *Deutschland* Panzergrenadier Regiment linked up with Peiper's kampfgruppe, that the German position in the town was fully secure. The Russians continued to harry Peiper's men in the town, and he was forced to conduct a number of panzer sweeps of the countryside to expand the German grip on the region. During one such operation a pair of Tiger I tanks were attacked by Russian tanks, who destroyed an accompanying armoured halftrack before they were driven off for the loss of 10 tanks, two armoured cars and 10 trucks.

Peiper's dash to Belgorod had been possible thanks to a return of winter weather, but in the final days of March the temperature was rising and the snow disappeared. It was replaced by deep mud, which made all movement off roads, even by tracked vehicles, almost impossible. The *Totenkopf* and *Das Reich* Divisions fought a series of bitter infantry battles to establish a firm frontline along the Donets, east of Kharkov, for several days, but the spring campaign season was all but over.

Back in Kharkov, Waffen-SS panzergrenadiers combed the ruins of the city for the few remaining pockets of Soviet troops, and were also settling some old scores with its citizens. The desecration of the graves of Waffen-SS men killed during the January battles, and the mutilation of the bodies, made the *Leibstandarte* very loath to show any quarter to captured Russian soldiers. Several hundred wounded Soviet soldiers were murdered when Dietrich's men occupied the city's military hospital. Any captured commissars or senior Russian officers were executed as a matter of routine, in line with Hitler's infamous "commissar order".

Special German Gestapo squads, SS Sonderkommando security units and Einsatzgruppen with mobile gas chambers followed close behind the victorious German troops, to ensure there was no repeat of February's uprising. An estimated 10,000 men, women and children perished during Hausser's short reign of terror in the city of Kharkov.

On 18 March, the German High Command claimed that 50,000 Russian soldiers had died during Manstein's counter-offensive, along with 19,594 taken prisoner and 1140 tanks and 3000 guns destroyed. An impressive total but, when compared to the 250,000 Germans lost at Stalingrad, it is clear that the Soviets benefited more from the Kharkov battles. The Russians, their military production in full swing, could also replace their losses more easily.

I SS Panzer Corps played a key part in this victory. It demonstrated that it was one of the world's foremost armoured formations, holding out against superior odds and then counterattacking with great skill and *élan*. Its success was not achieved cheaply, though. Some 11,500 Waffen-SS men were killed or wounded during the two-month campaign in the Ukraine. Some 4500 of these were borne by the *Leibstandarte*, emphasizing its key role at the centre of all the major battles of the campaign. Indeed, the majority of the casualties were in the combat units of the three Waffen-SS divisions. Not to be forgotten is the role of the *Wiking* Division serving with the First Panzer Army. It lost thousands of men in a series of small skirmishes, but was still able to take the offensive and defeat superior odds. The material strength of I SS Panzer Corps was badly affected by two months of battle. Its panzer regiments could only field less than half the number of tanks they had brought from France eight weeks before.

Manstein was justifiably dubbed "the saviour of the Eastern Front" for his efforts in turning back the Russian tide. Events later in the year would prove the Red Army's defeat was only a temporary setback. The antics of the Waffen-SS in Kharkov placed the final phase of the German counteroffensive under a cloud. Hausser's premature assault cost his corps thousands of casualties and allowed the Third Tank Army to escape through the weak German encirclement force. The butchery of the Waffen-SS after they broke into the city was not really remarkable – it was standard behaviour for a force that was in the vanguard of their Führer's murderous campaign to rid Europe of Jews and Bolsheviks.

This, of course, was irrelevant to Hitler, who in the weeks after Kharkov expressed a faith in the elite Waffen-SS divisions that knew no bounds. He declared I SS Panzer Corps to be "worth 20 Italian divisions". Of more importance to those divisions, though, was the Führer's express order to General Zeitzler, his Army Chief of Staff, that "we must see that the SS gets the necessary personnel". And, in preparation for the summer campaign season, they were also to be given priority when it came to delivery of the latest Panzer V Panther tanks, much to the annoyance of the army.

A combination of mud and exhaustion brought military operations to a halt on the Eastern Front in mid-March 1943. Both sides needed to reorganize and re-equip for the forthcoming campaign season.

Chapter 4
KURSK

II SS Panzer Corps during Operation Citadel, July 1943.

During July 1943, the eyes of the world were on a nondescript stretch of undulating steppe around the previously unknown Russian city of Kursk. The run-down and unremarkable city, however, would soon enter military history as the centre point of the most decisive battle of World War II. Here, the might of the German Wehrmacht would stage its last major strategic offensive of the war on the Eastern Front. The Red Army held its ground, and within weeks would stage its own massive counteroffensive that eventually drove all the way to the heart of the Third Reich, to Berlin itself. After Kursk, Stalin's armies would hold the strategic initiative on the Eastern Front.

In the build-up to the battle both sides massed their best troops, tanks, artillery and aircraft. By early July, the Germans had concentrated 43 divisions, with 2700 tanks and assault guns, supported by 1800 combat aircraft. Barring their way were 100 Russian divisions and five tank armies, with 3306 tanks and 2650 aircraft. Within days these gigantic war machines would clash to decide the fate of the world.

The origins of this titanic clash stretched back to the winter battles around Kharkov in February and March 1943. German counterattacks pushed back the Soviet spearheads that had surged westwards during the winter. By the time the spring thaw made all movement off roads impossible, the Wehrmacht had regained lost ground and stabilized the front. But the Soviets retained control of a huge salient that bulged more than 80km (50 miles) westwards into German-held territory.

To the German High Command, the 160km- (100-mile-) wide salient was a prize that could not be resisted. A rapid panzer advance, punching inwards from either shoulder of the salient, would trap hundreds of thousands of Russian troops and, in turn, shorten the German front. This would free more than 15 divisions and allow a new offensive to be mounted on the Eastern Front, one that would finally finish off Stalin's resistance once and for all. For Adolf Hitler, the proposed Kursk Offensive offered a chance to turn the tide of war in Germany's favour to counter growing Anglo-American power in the West (the campaign in North Africa had ended in Axis defeat in May 1943). If Russia could be defeated, then the might of the Wehrmacht could be turned westwards in time for the expected cross-Channel invasion in 1944. German success on the Eastern Front was also seen by the Führer as an essential gambit to keep key Axis allies – Romania, Hungary, Italy and Finland – fighting on Berlin's side. Hitler was also convinced that the raw materials

KURSK

and industrial resources of the Ukraine would be decisive in the "war of production" between the Axis and the Allies.

Hitler's generals were divided concerning how to proceed. His field commanders in the East wanted an immediate offensive in April, to exploit their victories around Kharkov and catch the Soviets before they had time to rebuild their strength. Others wanted to husband the precious panzer divisions and use them to launch a decisive counterstroke against the expected Soviet summer offensive, to capitalize on the Wehrmacht's experience and expertise in armoured warfare.

The Führer was at first undecided. As ever, he was keen to attack, but wanted any offensive to be a dramatic success which would signal that Germany was still the dominant military power in the world. For this reason he was determined to use Germany's newest "wonder weapons" to inflict a punishing defeat on the Red Army. The new 45.72-tonne (45-ton) Panzer V Panther tank and Ferdinand super-heavy assault guns/tank destroyers were to spearhead the attack. Hitler placed great store on the Panther, and repeatedly delayed the offensive to ensure that large numbers of the new tank would be ready to spearhead the assault operation. While preparations for the offensive began in April, it was not until the first days of July that Hitler gave the go-ahead.

The plan's strategic concept was essentially very simple. Colonel-General Walter Model's Ninth Army was to push southwards into the northern shoulder of the salient. At the same time, Field Marshal Erich von Manstein's Army Group South would strike northwards to link up with Model's men, trapping the Soviet defenders holding the line west of Kursk. Both attack forces were to contain strong armoured reserves, which would be on hand to defeat any Russian counterattacks. Operation

Citadel was to be a repeat of the classic Blitzkrieg victories of 1941–42, when huge Soviet armies had been encircled with ease by marauding panzer armies.

Model's assault force eventually grew to include some six army panzer divisions, two panzergrenadier divisions and 13 infantry divisions. Two battalions of the monster Ferdinands would spearhead an assault force that contained more than 700 tanks and 250 assault guns.

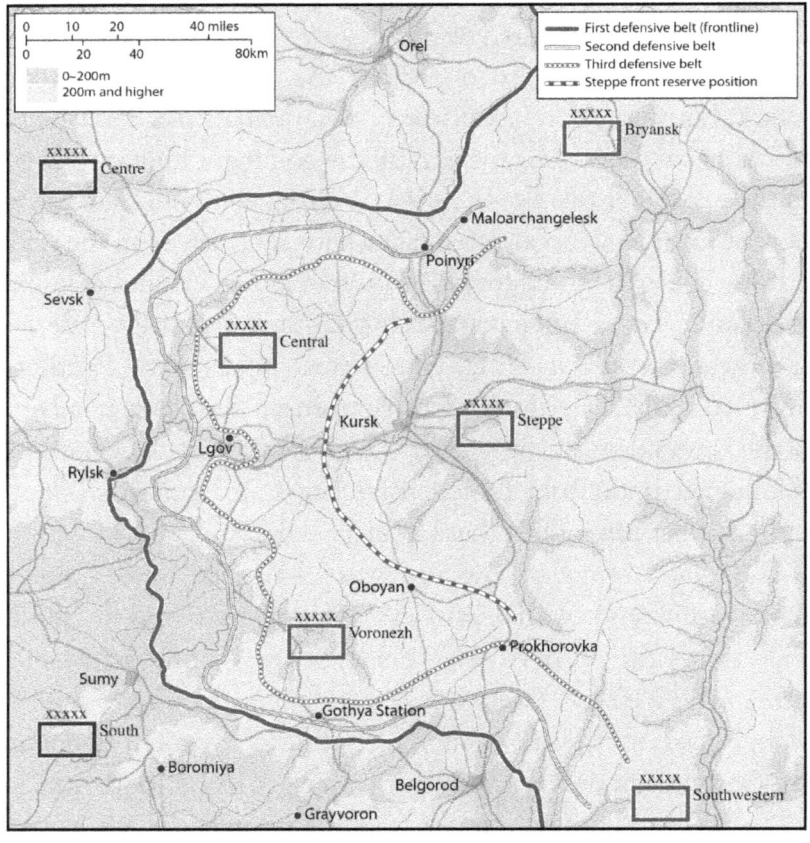

The Battle of Kursk: Soviet defensive belts

The most powerful elements of the German attack force, however, were concentrated on the southern axis, where Manstein had three army panzer corps and three infantry corps. He also had command of II SS Panzer Corps, which had grown into the most powerful tank formation on the European mainland, with 430 tanks and assault guns ready for action on the eve of battle. III and XXXXVIII Panzer Corps, of the Fourth Panzer Army, boasted more than 870 tanks and assault guns at the start of Operation Citadel, the codename of the German offensive. In reserve was XXIV Panzer Corps with another 150 tanks. In total, Manstein had amassed some 1500 armoured vehicles for the attack, including the first 200 Panthers which were formed into a special brigade to support the Army's *Grossdeutschland* Panzergrenadier Division.

The Luftwaffe built up a major force of tank-hunting aircraft to provide close air support to the assault troops. These assets included 37mm cannon-armed Junkers Ju 87G Stukas and 30mm cannon-armed Henschel Hs 129s. Manstein had more than 1000 Luftwaffe combat aircraft to support his offensive, and a string of radar stations were positioned around the southern flank of the salient to give prior warning of Russian air activity.

The surrender of 230,000 German troops in Tunisia in May to British and American forces stiffened Hitler's resolve to launch Operation Citadel. In his mind there was no time to spare before Anglo-American forces made landings on mainland Europe.

During the final days of March 1943, SS-Obergruppenführer Paul Hausser was able to finally pull his weary divisions out of the line to be rested and rebuilt. The *Leibstandarte, Das Reich* and *Totenkopf* Divisions were pulled back to billets in Kharkov and neighbouring towns, which only a few months before had been battlegrounds. There was little in the way of home comforts, but the Waffen-SS men had other things on their minds. A major reorganization of the corps was ordered by the Führer, who wanted to build up his beloved Waffen-SS so he would not have to rely on the army and its generals, who in his mind only seemed to want to retreat.

At the end of March, the Führer informed the *Leibstandarte* Division's commander, SS-Obergruppenführer Josef "Sepp" Dietrich, that his unit would be the core of a new corps, to be known as I SS Panzer Corps *Leibstandarte Adolf Hitler*. Scores of staff officer from Dietrich's division would form the new corps staff, while hundreds of officers and noncommissioned officers were to be drafted to form a training cadre to establish the new Hitler Youth SS panzergrenadier division. A number of artillery, assault gun and antitank battalions were also transferred from the *Leibstandarte* to the new division, to provide the core of its specialist regiments.

As a result of these developments, Hausser's formation was renamed II SS Panzer Corps, even though it was the first such headquarters to be set up by the Waffen-SS.

Preparations for the offensive

As trainloads of *Leibstandarte* veterans headed westwards, those who remained behind were ordered to prepare their units for action in a few weeks' time. Thousands of replacement soldiers were now arriving on a daily basis. These were mostly a mix of raw conscripts and drafted Luftwaffe ground personnel. Gone were the days when the Waffen-SS could pick and choose who served in its ranks. When Dietrich greeted the first batch of ex-Luftwaffe men in Kharkov, he asked for volunteers for the panzergrenadiers. There were few takers – most of the new Waffen-SS men wanted to serve in maintenance and repair teams. In future the replacements were not to be given a choice regarding which units they would serve in. Most of these recruits were directed to the *Leibstandarte* Division because of the heavy casualties it had suffered during the previous two months.

A constant stream of trains arrived at Kharkov with new tanks, artillery, vehicles and other equipment. Waffen-SS repair teams worked overtime to restore the scores of tanks damaged in action back to fighting condition. No one trusted them to be returned in time for the coming offensive if they were shipped back to workshops in Germany.

The panzer regiments of the Waffen-SS divisions were extensively reorganized to absorb their new equipment. The *Leibstandarte* and *Das Reich* Divisions were both ordered to send the first battalion of their panzer regiments back to Germany, for training in the use of the new Panther tank. This process would not be complete by the time Operation Citadel began, contrary to the many accounts of the Battle of Kursk which have stated that the Waffen-SS divisions fielded hundreds of the new tanks during the offensive. In fact, the Panther would not make its appearance on the Eastern Front in Waffen-SS service until the middle of August 1943.

The Waffen-SS was also not equipped with hundreds of Tiger I tanks at Kursk: only three companies of the heavy tanks saw service with II SS Panzer Corps during July 1943. Each division did have a battalion of Sturmgeschütz (StuG) III assault guns and a strong contingent of Marder III self-propelled antitank guns.

By the time Operation Citadel got under way, the *Leibstandarte*'s panzer regiment boasted one battalion, with 67 Panzer IV and 13

Panzer III tanks, along with 13 Tiger Is. The *Das Reich* Division was less well equipped, with only 33 Panzer IVs, 62 Panzer IIIs and 14 Tiger Is. To boost its fighting power, the division pressed 25 captured T-34s into service. The *Totenkopf* Division still had two battalions in its panzer regiment, but 63 of its tanks were Panzer IIIs. It also had 44 heavier Panzer IVs and 15 Tiger Is.

The *Wiking* Division's panzer unit had been upgraded to regimental status, however it had yet to grow beyond battalion strength. In July 1943 it could only muster 23 Panzer III and 17 Panzer IV tanks. It had no Tigers, and was kept in reserve throughout the Kursk Offensive.

To further increase the firepower of Hausser's corps, the army provided two heavy artillery and two rocket launcher regiments, as well as a special command headquarters to coordinate fire missions of all artillery units in the corps. This meant that huge amounts of firepower could be brought down on individual targets in a very short space of time.

To prepare his command for battle, Hausser ordered a series of training exercises to be held. Noncommissioned officers drilled the new recruits to turn them into combat soldiers. Tank driving and gunnery courses were run on the new vehicles and weapons being delivered to the Waffen-SS. Senior commanders were given top-secret briefings on the Operation Citadel plan, and were shown scores of Luftwaffe aerial photographs of the Soviet defences in their respective sectors.

Company and battalion field exercises were held on the steppe around Kharkov to familiarize the troops with equipment and practice the tactics to be used during the coming battle. Finally, divisional and corps "command post" exercises were put on to acquaint the Waffen-SS commanders and staff officers with the plan. They based their planning on intelligence that said four Russian infantry divisions were holding the enemy's first defensive line in II SS Panzer Corps' sector. Two more held the second line, and behind them were two tank corps with at least 360 tanks. After defeating these forces, counterattacks were to be expected from several more enemy tank corps. Although many Waffen-SS men were superbly confident regarding their own equipment and abilities – arrogance was a common trait among Hitler's "master race" – some of the older veterans knew the coming battle would be like no other they had previously faced.

By the end of June, II SS Panzer Corps was warned to be ready to move forward to its assembly area in a few days. The Führer decided on 21 June – almost two years to the day since the start of his invasion of Russia – to launch the operation on 5 July. On 1 July Hitler called his senior commanders to his headquarters in East Prussia to receive a final "pep talk". There was now no turning back. The Waffen-SS divisions started to move from their billets around Kharkov to their assembly areas near Belgorod in a series of night-time road moves. During daylight hours they remained out of sight in forests, waiting for X-Day, as the start day of the operation was codenamed, to dawn.

On the other side of the frontline, Marshal of the Soviet Union Georgi Zhukov was ready and waiting for the German offensive. The victor of the battles of Moscow and Stalingrad also recognized the importance of the Kursk salient, and so was not prepared to give it up lightly. He knew the Germans would attack, and saw the chance to engage their precious panzer divisions in a war of attrition. Once they had been worn down, he would launch his reserves in a massive offensive along the whole length of the Eastern Front, to inflict a strategic defeat of such magnitude that the Third Reich would not be able to recover from it.

Zhukov was appointed to coordinate the defence of Kursk, and he was given unlimited resources to do the job. Unknown to the Soviet commander, his biggest help came from his British allies, who for three years had been reading all of the Third Reich's secret radio communications traffic. The British had broken the Germans' Enigma code using an early form of computer, but they were unwilling to reveal to Stalin the full extent of their code-breaking success, and so created a convoluted means to pass so-called "Ultra" material to Moscow. This involved establishing contact with a ring of Soviet agents in Switzerland, codenamed Lucy, and drip-feeding them Ultra decodes relevant to the war in Russia. The Lucy agents were convinced they were receiving documents from disgruntled German officers within Hitler's inner circle. The result was that within days Moscow had verbatim transcripts of high-level orders being sent from Hitler's headquarters to his senior commanders on the Eastern Front. These included all the plans for Operation Citadel, including details of units, objectives, logistic information and, most crucially, the date for the start of the offensive. Hitler's desire to micro-manage the war down to the lowest level played into the Soviets' hands. They knew the every move of almost all German units, often before the commanders of those units themselves. Indeed, Manstein's success during the Kharkov Offensive has been attributed to the fact that he did not consult the Führer on many of his moves, so they were not compromised to the Lucy Ring and thus caught Red Army commanders by surprise.

With this vital information in his hip pocket, Zhukov was able to plan his defence in a methodical way. Nothing would be left to chance. The key to Zhukov's plan was the need to prevent the German panzers from breaking free and manoeuvring against the Soviet rear areas. He recognized that Soviet units were inferior to the Germans when it came to mobile warfare, and he wanted to close down the battle into a series of local set-piece actions. A network of strong-points, each reinforced with scores of antitank guns, were built around the Kursk salient. Each strong-point was mutually supporting, so once the Germans attacked one they would be raked by well-aimed fire from another. The Germans were to be given no chance to put their mobile Blitzkrieg tactics into action, especially rampaging into the rear of Soviet formations and positions. Zhukov wanted to capitalize on his soldiers' dogged determination in defensive operations. He wanted to trade their lives and their antitank guns for panzers. Russia had a massive supply of men and hardware at this stage of the war, while Germany could never hope to replace its panzer divisions, which had been rebuilt after the disaster at Stalingrad, if they were decimated once more. This was to be the Verdun of the Eastern Front – a brutal battle of attrition rather than a fast-moving tank battle.

For three months the Russians poured men and machines into the Kursk salient to build a string of defence lines almost 48km (30 miles) deep. Millions of mines were laid along the length of the salient, and behind them thousands of antitank guns and artillery pieces were sited in hundreds of strong-points. Positioned between the defence lines were tank brigades, ready to launch immediate counterattacks, and behind the four main defence lines were tank corps held in reserve to seal any German breakthroughs. Hundreds of kilometres to the rear was the Fifth Guards Tank Army, Zhukov's strategic reserve, which was being held ready to deliver the *coup de grâce* against the German offensive. Once committed, the Soviet strategic reserve would decide the fate of the war on the Eastern Front.

In II SS Panzer Corps' sector, the Soviet Sixth Guards Army created what was intended to be a death trap for the Waffen-SS men. Facing the brunt of the German attack were the soldiers of the 67th and 52nd Guards Rifle Divisions. They manned a series of strong-points along a ridge line, which allowed them to observe the approach routes to the southern shoulder of the Kursk salient and call down massive barrages of artillery and multi-barrel Katyusha rocket launcher (the so-called Stalin's Organ) fire on German assembly areas. Two antitank regiments and two tank regiments were spread out among the first-echelon divisions to stiffen their resistance. The tanks and antitank guns were emplaced in bunkers to protect them from shell fire. Along the front was some 290km (181 miles) of trench lines. Hundreds of kilometres of antitank ditches were dug to channel the German attack towards antitank killing zones. More than 1000 machine-gun nests and mortar batteries were positioned to cover the mine belts, to stop German combat engineers clearing paths through the 140,000 mines. Some 300 pillboxes and over 3000 individual bunkers protected several thousand riflemen and tank-hunting squads armed with antitank rifles. Some 9.6km (six miles) behind the main defence line were three infantry divisions, a tank brigade and two more regiments of antitank guns. They had prepared similarly strong defence lines to their comrades in the frontline, although the mine belts were thinner with only 30,000 mines. Throughout the Sixth Guards Army's sector, there were more than 400 antitank guns between 45mm and

76mm calibre, some 778 mortars and almost 500 artillery pieces between 76mm and 203mm calibre. They were all in prepared positions, and their target-spotting teams had had three months to pre-register ranges and targets.

Nearly 48km (30 miles) behind the front were the so-called rear-defence lines, which were sited on a number of key rivers, blocking the advance to Kursk itself. These contained a far higher density of mines, machine guns, mortars and antitank guns than

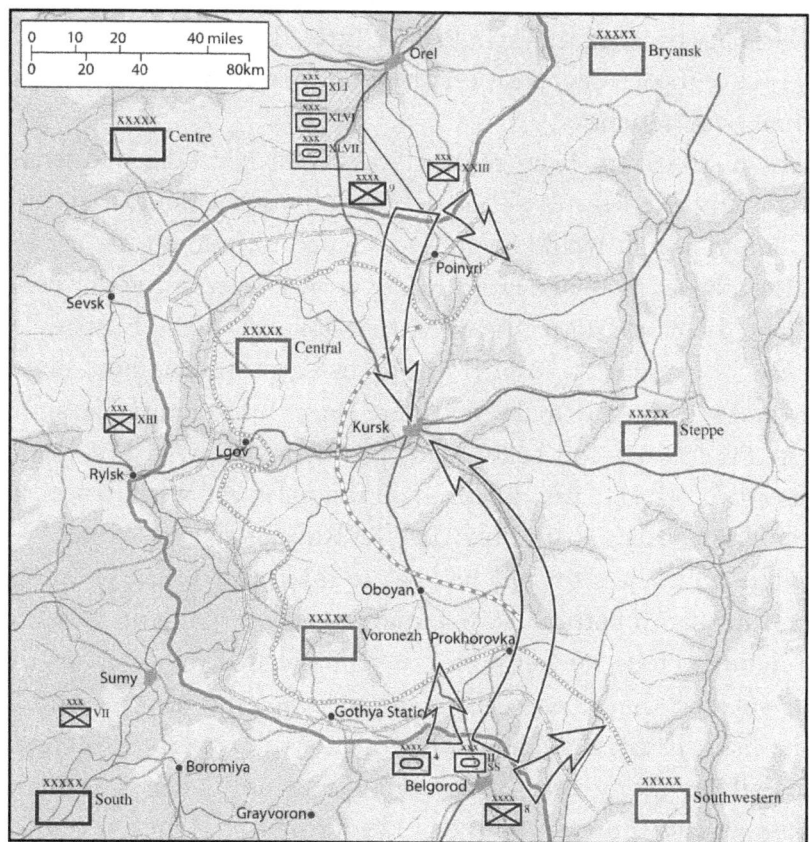

The Battle of Kursk: German plans

in the second line. Not content with this density of fortification, Zhukov ordered another defensive sector – of three lines – to be build at the base of salient, in case the Germans punched through the initial defence lines. To add to the Germans' problems, all the construction work on the Soviet defensive positions was to be conducted at night or under camouflage nets so Luftwaffe photographic reconnaissance would not be able to pinpoint them. Hundreds of dummy trench lines, bunkers and minefields were also prepared to confuse German intelligence. When the Germans attacked they would have little idea of the real tactical layout of the Russian positions, beyond what they could see from their own trenches.

From the Lucy Ring reports and tactical intelligence from prisoners and deserters, Zhukov knew almost the hour when the German assault would begin. He seemed to hold all the cards. The wily Soviet commander, however, was far from complacent. Once the battle started he knew that anything could happen.

By the evening of 3 July, II SS Panzer Corps was deployed in its assembly areas and final orders were issued for the initial assault. On the left was the *Leibstandarte*, in the centre was *Das Reich* and the *Totenkopf* was deployed on the right. All were to attack simultaneously to batter through the Russian defence lines.

The attack was to start just before midnight on the evening of 4 July, with battalion-sized infantry assaults going in to seize a number of key Soviet positions to allow artillery observers to be sited so they could call in fire to cover the attack against the main Russian defence line. Soviet artillery barrages started to fall on the Waffen-SS divisions' assembly areas just after dusk, causing minor casualties and confusion, but they were not intense enough to stop the main attack. The first attacks went in on schedule, with small groups of panzergrenadiers infiltrating through minefields and rushing the enemy trenches. In two hours of hand-to-hand combat, the outposts were captured and the main attack of the *Leibstandarte* Division was ready to roll at just after dawn – 04:05 hours – on 5 July.

Each of the division's panzergrenadier regiments was given a major Russian strong-point as an objective. The Waffen-SS panzer regiments and armoured troop-carrier battalions were kept in reserve to exploit any breakthrough created by the panzergrenadiers. For 50 minutes before the attack the massed artillery of the corps blasted the objectives, and in the final five minutes of the barrage Junkers Ju 87 Stuka dive-bombers joined the attack. The bombardment demolished whole sections of trench line and scores of antitank guns, stunning the Russian defenders. Once the *Leibstandarte*'s attack was under way, the artillery and Stuka support was switched to "soften up" the defences in front of the *Das Reich* Division, which was due to attack at 08:15 hours.

Tiger Is, StuG IIIs and Marders then rolled forward with the first wave of panzergrenadiers to give them close support as they moved into action. This was the so-called panzerkeil, or wedge, tactic. The presence of the armoured firepower was the key to the success of the assault, with the Tigers and other vehicles acting as mobile pillboxes. They destroyed scores of machine-gun nests in quick succession to allow the panzergrenadier assault teams to move in to clear out the trench lines with hand grenades and flamethrowers. Dozens of antitank guns were destroyed by the giant tanks, which were impervious to Soviet fire. These assault operations took until well into the afternoon, and cost the *Leibstandarte* Division some 500 casualties alone. The close-quarter fighting was vicious and few Soviet soldiers showed any inclination to surrender, with just over 100 being captured by the Waffen-SS during the day. By mid-afternoon, the *Leibstandarte* and *Das Reich* Divisions were ready to start the next phase of the operation: launching their panzer reserves forward. *Das Reich's* panzers got stuck in a previously undiscovered minefield, and the *Leibstandarte's* surged ahead until they ran into the pak-front of the Soviet 28th Anti-Tank Brigade. Two Tigers were damaged by the expertly dug-in antitank guns, before the *Leibstandarte's* commanders ordered the advance halted until infantry could be brought up during the night to clear out the enemy's second-line defences.

The *Leibstandarte* and *Das Reich* Divisions were the most successful units on the German southern wing on the first day of the offensive. Their army comrades on each wing got bogged down in the thick mud and the numerous Soviet minefields.

Throughout the night, the Waffen-SS commanders reorganized their forces to punch through the second line of enemy defences as soon as it got light. Again a massive artillery and rocket launcher bombardment was planned, to be followed by an infantry assault with Tiger tank support. It took almost two hours for the *Leibstandarte's* panzergrenadiers to clear paths through the Soviet mine belts and blow holes in the barbed-wire entanglements. Daylight came, and in four more hours of fighting the Waffen-SS men cleared out the enemy bunkers and gun positions.

Meanwhile, the *Das Reich's Der Führer* Panzergrenadier Regiment was repulsed with heavy losses when it tried to take a strong-point in its sector. A divisional-sized artillery fire mission was needed to clear the way forward.

KURSK

SS-Standartenführer Theodor Wisch, the *Leibstandarte*'s new commander, was forward in his armoured halftrack watching the battle, and once the panzergrenadiers had cleared a passage through the enemy position he gave orders for his panzer kampfgruppe to motor northwards. It had barely moved a few hundred metres forward when more than 45 T-34s charged out of a wood directly at the Waffen-SS tanks. Eight were knocked out by the panzers, while Stuka dive-bombers picked off another three before the Soviet tanks retreated. The panzers were rearmed and refuelled in the forward battle zone from halftrack supply vehicles before moving forward again later in the afternoon, with panzergrenadiers providing support in armoured carriers. They only got a few kilometres northwards before the force ran into a massive pak-front and huge minefield. Four tanks and many halftracks were lost to mines. At the same time as the *Leibstandarte* Division's panzers were rolling forward, *Das Reich*'s panzer kampfgruppe and reconnaissance battalion were ordered to exploit the breach created by their own panzergrenadiers. They destroyed 10 Soviet tanks, but were stropped in their tracks by antitank fire which hit a number of Tigers. Again the Soviets had managed to halt the German attack and prevent the panzers breaking into the open countryside.

Out on the Waffen-SS right flank, the *Totenkopf* Division was still battling to cut through the 52nd Guards Rifle Division, which was tenaciously holding its main defence position during most of the morning. Attacks in the late morning broke the back of the defence, though, and the *Totenkopf* was able to make big gains. However, in the afternoon large Soviet counterattacks by II Guards Tank Corps battered the division's right flank. Wave after wave of tanks surged forward, with some attacks involving more than 300 Soviet tanks.

During the night of 6 July, the Russians reinforced V Guards Tank Corps opposite with three brigades in preparation for a major counterattack against the Waffen-SS. Small probing attacks were launched in the dawn light by individual tanks, supported by squads of tank-riding infantry. At 06:00 hours the *Leibstandarte* and *Das Reich* panzer kampfgruppen were ordered forward. In the morning gloom Soviet tank brigades attacked the Waffen-SS panzers from three sides. They surged forward in waves, to be hit by a wall of fire from the German panzers. The main assault wave was made up of dozens of T-34s. They were picked off one-by-one by the panzers, but still kept attacking. The *Leibstandarte*'s Tiger company was in the thick of the action, alone accounting for more than 30 T-34s.

In spite of their terrible losses, the Soviet tanks were soon among the German formations. Panzergrenadiers picked off those tanks that came close and shot any tank-riding infantry on their hulls. The battle raged all day. More than 90 tanks and 60 artillery pieces were lost and 600 Russians were captured in the battle, which decimated XXXI Tank Corps and III Mechanized Corps. Their actions, however, successfully blocked the German advance into the heart of the Soviet third defence line.

The tank dogfight between the Waffen-SS and Russian T-34 crews continued overnight and into the morning of 8 July. Soviet tank attacks were an almost hourly occurrence. Whole battalions and brigades of T-34s would suddenly appear from forests and villages to charge the panzer kampfgruppen, which were at the tip of a 19.2km- (12-mile-) deep breach in Soviet lines gouged out by II SS Panzer Corps.

The *Leibstandarte* and *Das Reich* panzer kampfgruppen moved around the exposed steppe, destroying dozens of Soviet tanks with their long-range weapons. To increase the firepower available, the *Leibstandarte*'s assault gun battalion was moved up to the spearhead of the division.

The panzers and assault guns could not be everywhere, though, and individual Russians tanks easily penetrated the thinly stretched defences of the *Das Reich*'s and *Leibstandarte*'s panzergrenadier regiments. Antitank guns and hand grenades drove off most of the Russian attacks. Four T-34s managed to sneak through the German defences, and get within a few hundred metres of the *Leibstandarte*'s divisional headquarters, before they were knocked out by tank-hunting teams armed with hollow-charge mines.

Hausser was singularly determined to press forward the attack, and so, just before midday, the *Leibstandarte* and *Das Reich* armoured kampfgruppen were ordered to wheel northwestwards. Their objective was to seize the crossings over the River Psel and breach the Russian third line, thus opening a clear route northwards.

The panzers, led by the *Leibstandarte*'s Tigers, destroyed 22 T-34s as they moved across the open steppe towards the river. As the assault groups approached the Psel valley, they ran into an antitank brigade hidden among the villages and woods along the valley. A network of mines and bunkers forced the panzer commanders to rein in their tanks. A small squad of *Das Reich*'s panzergrenadiers did score a major success when they infiltrated through a minefield and captured a Soviet divisional command post and a general. The Soviet defence did not crack, though, and the German drive north had been blocked.

Over on the eastern flank, the *Leibstandarte*'s assault gun battalion led a panzergrenadier attack northeastwards, which allowed several villages to be cleared of isolated pockets of Soviet infantry.

By the evening of 8 July, the two lead Waffen-SS divisions had destroyed more than 120 tanks, but 76 of their panzers were badly in need of repairs. Many of the panzer companies were down to half strength, and time was needed to patch up the scores of battle-damaged tanks that were filling up the repair workshops.

As the battle raged on at the *schwerpunkt*, Hausser put in train plans to relieve the *Totenkopf* Division and move it up to punch a hole through the defences along the Psel. The *Totenkopf* Division had been holding the right flank of II SS Panzer Corps since the start of the offensive, and it spent most of the day handing over its sector to an army infantry division. However, the safe completion of this manoeuvre was only possible thanks to the intervention of the Luftwaffe.

During the morning, three cannon-armed Hs 129 tank-hunting aircraft were patrolling to the east of the *Totenkopf*, when they spotted a Soviet tank brigade of 60 T-34s forming up ready to smash into the flank of the Waffen-SS corps. More aircraft were summoned and, in less than an hour, the whole brigade was either destroyed by 30mm cannon fire, or forced to scatter into woods and gullies to hide from the aircraft. The attack totally disrupted the preparations of II Guards Tank Corps to pressurize the *Totenkopf*, allowing the Waffen-SS unit to successfully disengage from the front.

The first regiment of the *Totenkopf* Division was in position ready to attack the Psel line early after dawn on 9 July, along with the *Leibstandarte*'s 1st Panzergrenadier Regiment. It didn't have enough strength to punch through the heavily reinforced Soviet defence line, though. A bridge across the Psel had been blown to prevent a crossing. By mid-afternoon, the Waffen-SS attack had been called off to allow preparations to be made for a more substantial attack the following day. The *Totenkopf* made a night-time raid to seize a key hill above the Psel, but it was driven back. The Soviets kept up their pressure on the right flank of Hausser's corps, sending repeated human-wave attacks against the 167th Infantry Division that had just relieved the *Totenkopf*. Thousands of Russian infantrymen, many of them press-ganged civilians, were mown down by well-aimed artillery fire that was called down within a few hundred metres of the German frontline.

The Soviets were also feeling the strain of battle by this time. Their third line of defence was holding up – but only just. Zhukov had committed all his local reserves. A final decision was now made to commit the strategic reserve. The three tanks corps of the Fifth Guards Tank Army received orders to move westwards to engage the Waffen-SS, and stop them taking a town called Prokhorovka. It would take them three days to be in a position to strike. In the meantime, the troops at the front would have to hold on.

Manstein also realized that the battle was approaching a critical point, and had prepared orders for XXXXIV Panzer Corps, led by the *Wiking* Division, to start towards Belgorod to exploit any breakthrough by Hausser's spearheads. Reports from the northern shoulder of the Kursk salient were not encouraging. The German offensive was stalled, and Soviet troops were even starting to drive forward.

Amid heavy summer rain showers, II SS Panzer Corps moved forward again in a coordinated attack to crack open the final line of Russian resistance. The *Totenkopf* Division was now fully deployed to the left of the *Leibstandarte*, and it was launched forward to seize a bridgehead across the Psel. The *Theodor Eicke* Panzergrenadier Regiment led the attack, which was preceded by heavy artillery fire. Assault guns provided close support as the panzergrenadiers stormed the heavily defended villages along the Psel. The Soviet XXXIII Rifle Corps held out for the morning, trading artillery and mortar fire with the Germans, as well as launching a number of counterattacks. *Totenkopf* commanders led their men forward again in the afternoon, and two bridgeheads were established. It took several hours before bridging equipment could be brought up to allow armour to cross the swollen Psel, to press home the advance. Heavy rain delayed the work, which meant the bridge would not be ready to carry tanks for another day.

Consolidating the bridgehead

More artillery was brought forward to soften up the Russians to allow the *Totenkopf* to expand its bridgeheads. Stukas joined the assault during the afternoon, and by early evening a third breach had been made in the Soviet defence line. At nightfall three Waffen-SS panzergrenadier battalions were over the Psel, and they held off repeated counterattacks as darkness approached.

On the main road to Prokhorovka, the *Leibstandarte*'s 2nd Panzergrenadier Regiment, reinforced with Tigers, assault guns and Marders, prepared for a dawn attack. Panzers, reconnaissance troops and infantry in armoured halftracks stood ready to exploit the breach. All the division's artillery regiment, backed by rocket launchers and Stukas, pounded the Soviet defence lines on a wooded hill. A battle raged on the slopes and in the woods between Waffen-SS panzergrenadiers and Soviet infantrymen. Soviet artillery joined in the battle, directed from the hills along the northern bank of the Psel. The accurate shell fire brought the *Leibstandarte*'s casualties up to over 200 for the day. Dug-in T-34s had to be destroyed individually by the Tigers, to allow the hill to be taken by the late afternoon. More than 50 Soviet tanks were knocked out and 23 assault guns destroyed. By the time darkness returned to the battlefield, there was still no breakthrough and the panzer kampfgruppe had still to be deployed.

To the south, the *Das Reich* Division was ordered to strike eastwards to seize high ground overlooking the main positions of the Waffen-SS corps. The *Deutschland* Panzergrenadier Regiment made some progress at first, but very strong antitank resistance prevented much progress being made thereafter.

Soviet counterattacks on the Psel bridgehead opened at 08:00 hours on 11 July with a heavy tank attack that was driven off by the *Totenkopf*'s antitank gunners, who knocked out 27 Russian tanks. This allowed work to continue on the bridge, which was capable of carrying the heavy Tiger tanks. Heavy rain and Soviet shelling continued to hamper the work of the Waffen-SS engineers, who did not finish their work until just before midday. The division's 94 tanks then began to cross the river, and plans were put in motion for a major offensive the following day. Victory seemed to be within sight.

The *Leibstandarte* pushed forward again to take the last hill-top pak-front before Prokhorovka. Two panzergrenadier battalions led the attack on the hill, which was bristling with antitank guns. They laid down a withering wall of fire which stalled the

Waffen-SS attack. Then a wave of T-34s was sent into action against the Germans.

Rocket fire and Stuka support was requested to neutralize the resistance in a barrage that began at 09:00 hours. The air support was directed with great precision by a Luftwaffe forward air controller in an armoured halftrack with the attack troops. The arrival of a detachment of Tiger attacks added to the weight of the assault. Within the hour, the panzergrenadiers

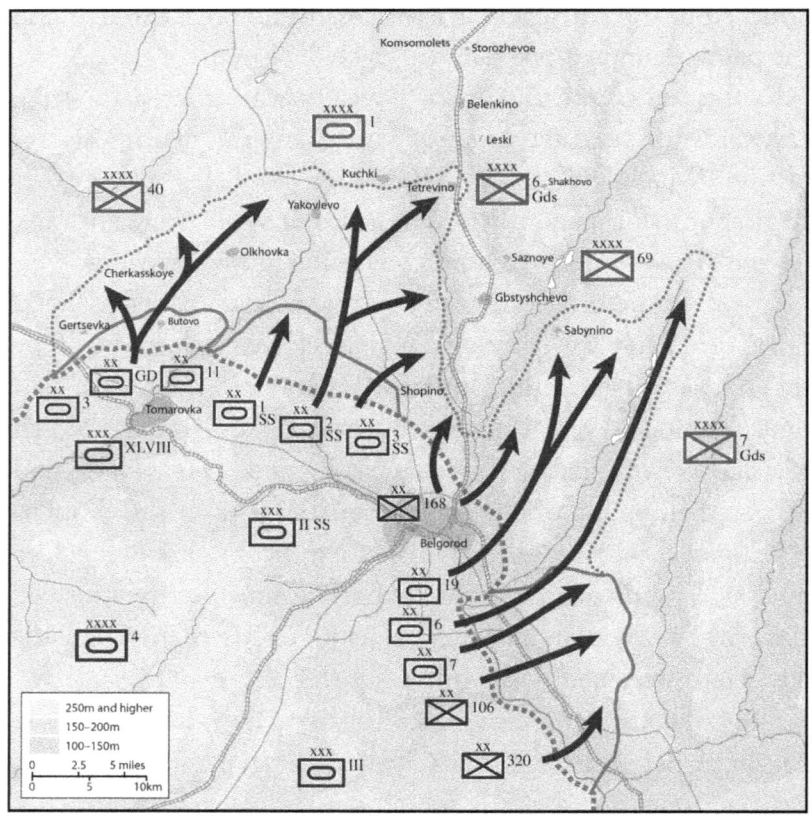

The Battle of Kursk: Southern front, 4–7 July 1943

had penetrated the Russian trench system and were clearing bunker after bunker. The fighting flowed back and forth as the Russians threw more men into that battle. Stuka raids continued throughout the morning.

Now the *Leibstandarte* panzer kampfgruppe was thrown into the battle, and this turned the tide in the Germans' favour for good. Soviet tank counterattacks against the flanks of the *Leibstandarte* were repulsed. The Russians lost 21 tanks and more than 30 antitank guns. More than 200 Waffen-SS men were killed or wounded during the bitter fighting for the hill. This degenerated into a tank duel along the length of the division's front, involving attacks by small groups of tanks.

The final Waffen-SS assault

Satisfied with their success over the Psel and in front of Prokhorovka, Hausser's staff now set about planning the following day's drive to complete the piercing of the Soviet third defence line. More artillery was to be brought up to blast the Russians out of their bunkers on the hill above the *Totenkopf*'s bridgehead. Once this was complete, the *Leibstandarte* and *Das Reich* Divisions would surge forward to seize Prokhorovka. With the resistance destroyed, the panzers were to be unleashed into the open country beyond.

The Waffen-SS panzer regiments were rested during the night to prepare them for the coming major attack. Repair teams worked to ensure the maximum number of panzers were available. During the evening the *Leibstandarte* mustered five Panzer IIIs, 47 Panzer IVs and four Tiger Is ready for action; *Das Reich* fielded 34 Panzer IIIs, 18 Panzer IVs, one Tiger I and eight captured T-34s; and the *Totenkopf* had operational 54 Panzer

IIIs, 30 Panzer IVs and 10 Tiger Is. II SS Panzer Corps was also able to field 60 StuG IIIs and a similar number of Marder self-propelled antitank guns. In total, Hausser would have more than 300 armoured vehicles available for action.

He and his staff were convinced they were only a few hours away from achieving the decisive breakthrough and ultimate victory on the Eastern Front. They had no idea that only a few kilometres from the *Leibstandarte*'s advance posts, a force of more than 800 tanks and assault guns were massing to strike at them the following morning.

Marshal Pavel Rotmistrov had just led his Fifth Guards Tank Army on a 320km (200-mile) road march to Prokhorovka, and had spent the day preparing to launch it into action. He brought with him the fresh XVIII and XXIX Tank Corps and the Fifth Guards Mechanized Corps. To bolster his attack wave, he was assigned II Tank Corps or II Guards Tank Corps, which had already been blooded in the past week's clashes with the Waffen-SS. This force included 500 T-34s, with the remainder being light T-70s or lend-lease British Churchill and American General Lee tanks. Rotmistrov was Stalin's most experienced tank commander, and he set about preparing his mammoth tank force for action with great professionalism. The road march was accomplished in conditions of great secrecy under heavy fighter cover, and when his tanks halted to rest and refuel they were hidden in forest assembly areas. They gathered in the gullies and forests to the east and north of Prokhorovka under the cover of darkness, and awaited their orders.

Their commander recognized that, tank crew for tank crew, his men were no match for their German opponents. Only a few months before, many of his men had been the factory

KURSK

workers who had built the tanks and then driven them to the front. Rotmistrov realized that once under way, his force would soon run out of control. Most Soviet tanks did not have radios, and commanders controlled their subordinates by means of coloured flags. Therefore, Rotmistrov gave his corps and brigade commanders simple orders to follow, consisting of little more than specific objectives and axes of advance. The main way he could influence the battle was by tightly controlling the timing of when he committed his tank brigades, so the Soviet marshal set up his forward command post on a hill southwest of Prokhorovka, from where he could see all the key terrain and get a "finger tip" feel for the course of the battle. The Soviet marshal spent most of the night making final preparations for the mass attack, which was to start just after 06:00 hours the following morning, 12 July.

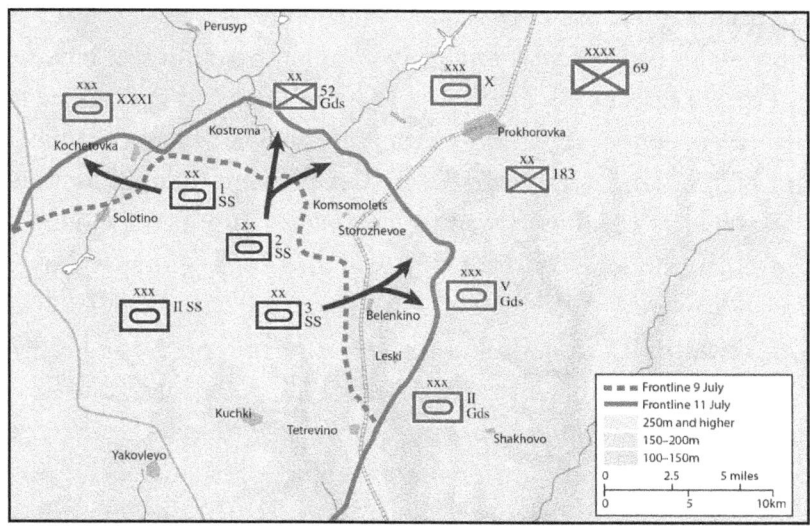

The Battle of Kursk: Southern front, 9–11 July 1943

The Battle of Prokhorovka effectively took place in an area little more than 8km by 8km (five miles by five miles) – it was smaller than the battlefield at Waterloo. The terrain where the main engagement of the battle was to unfold was flat and rolling. The main Waffen-SS tank forces were concentrated on a hill 1.6km (one mile) southwest of Prokhorovka. The ground gently slopped down towards the town, but then a small ridge line created an area of dead ground, behind which Rotmistrov had concentrated his main tank strike forces – XVIII and XXIX Tank Corps. A railway line and embankment, running southwest from Prokhorovka, created a natural division of the battlefield, meaning the Russians had to employ two distinct axes of attack. The railway line also formed the divisional boundary between the *Leibstandarte*, north of it, and *Das Reich*, to its south.

To the northwest of this gladiatorial arena was the River Psel, and the high ground on the northern bank of the river dominated the assembly area of the main Waffen-SS assault force – the *Leibstandarte* Division. The high ground was far too distant for direct tank fire from it to be a threat, but it provided a superb artillery observation vantage point. Whoever controlled this high ground dominated the battlefield. The valley along the Psel, with its small woods and villages, also provided a covered approach route to infiltrate behind the high ground above Prokhorovka.

Running south from Prokhorovka was a series of forested hills, running in a north-south direction, which were intersected by deep gullies and streams, making them poor ground for tanks.

Above the Psel, infantry battalions of the Soviet XXXI Tank Corps, without tank support, kicked off the Russian offensive by attacking during the night. The *Totenkopf* Division saw

KURSK

off the attack after hand-to-hand fighting in the villages around its bridgehead. In the face of heavy Soviet artillery, air raids and Stalin's Organ rocket fire, the *Totenkopf* Division's panzergrenadiers began their attack as scheduled just after dawn. The division's panzer regiment was now over the River Psel, and was poised to strike out once a route through the Soviet defences became apparent. Elements of the *Totenkopf*'s panzer kampfgruppe were committed at 07:15 hours, and they helped punch a first hole in the Soviet line.

All during the night, the forward outposts of the *Leibstandarte* were sending back reports to their headquarters, saying they were hearing noise from large numbers of tanks. In places Soviets tanks tried to probe the German line and, as dawn broke, scores of Russian fighter-bombers attacked the division's frontline positions, artillery fire bases and supply columns. It was becoming clear that something was wrong, but the Germans had no idea what it was. The division's panzer kampfgruppe was ordered to proceed with its early morning attack directly towards Prokhorovka, with the Tiger tank company in the lead. The *Das Reich*'s *Deutschland* Panzergrenadier Regiment was lined up as well, ready to advance northwards on the south side of the *Leibstandarte*.

Almost like clockwork, at 06:30 hours both the *Leibstandarte*'s panzers and the Soviet XXIX Tank Corps were waved forward by their commanders. In the morning haze, the Waffen-SS panzer crews spotted a mass of tanks 4.8–6.4km (3–4 miles) directly in front of them, on the far side of the valley. Some 60 tanks – a whole brigade of XXIX Tank Corps – were heading straight for them. Artillery fire and Katyusha rockets started to land among the German tanks. At the extreme limit of their range – 2000m

(6562ft) – the 50 or so Waffen-SS tanks started to pick-off the Soviet tanks. Rotmistrov had briefed his tank commanders not to stop to trade fire with the Germans, but to charge at full speed to make it more difficult to be hit, and to allow them to get into a position to hit the enemy tanks at close quarters on their more vulnerable side armour. The charge of the T-34s was a death ride. The Russian crews followed their orders to the letter, but by 09:00 hours the steppe was littered with burning hulks. The *Leibstandarte* tank crews had destroyed their enemy for almost no loss thanks to their long-range gunnery skills.

Rotmistrov's first wave also hit the *Das Reich* Division, with a brigade of XXIX Tank Corps taking a pounding from the *Leibstandarte*'s artillery as it moved forward. Then the *Das Reich* panzers put down withering fire to halt their attack. Rotmistrov now started to launch his brigades forward on an hourly basis in an attempt to batter through the German lines.

Next on the receiving end of an attack from XVIII Tank Corps was the *Totenkopf*'s *Theodor Eicke* Panzergrenadier Regiment in the Psel valley. Two Soviet infantry regiments backed by 50 tanks, pushed forward into the *Totenkopf*'s right flank at 07.:45 hours, to be seen off by the division's assault gun battalion.

At almost the same time, artillery and rocket fire rained down on the *Leibstandarte*'s 1st Panzergrenadier Regiment, which was holding the ground to the right of the division's panzer kampfgruppe. After an hour of softening-up artillery fire, the Russian armour was sent into action. The defenders were given a warning from a Luftwaffe reconnaissance patrol that a tank brigade was approaching along the railway line. Some 40 T-34s of XXIX Tank Corps were then among the German trenches. More were following behind in a second wave, along with hordes of Red infantry. Waffen-SS tank-hunting teams went to work taking on the Russian vehicles, but it took the intervention of five Marder self-propelled guns to see off the tanks.

Farther to the east, the *Leibstandarte*'s panzers were now attacked from two directions by more than 70 tanks of XVIII Tank Corps. An advance guard of seven panzers was overrun in the charge, losing four tanks to point-blank fire as the T-34s surged past them. The remaining three panzers were ignored by the Russian tanks, who were now heading directly for the main panzer kampfgruppe. The "lost" panzers turned to follow the T-34s, picking off 20 of them before the main panzer line opened fire with a mass volley. Stunned by the sudden burst of fire, the Russians halted to trade fire with the Germans. The 33 tanks of the panzer kampfgruppe now counterattacked, moving into flanking positions and raking the mass of confused Russian tanks with gunfire. After three hours of swirling action, the Germans claimed to have knocked out 62 T-70s and T-34s.

The *Totenkopf* Division continued to be pressed by XVIII Tank Corps, which committed its 32nd Motorized Infantry Brigade at 10:00 hours to another battle in the Psel valley. Some 50 tanks, including T-34s, T-70s and Churchills, were again driven off by the *Totenkopf*, which claimed 20 kills. At almost hourly intervals, Soviet infantry attacks were launched against all sides of the *Totenkopf*'s bridgehead to keep the pressure on the German left flank. Harassing artillery fire was also regularly directed at the two tank bridges to try to prevent reinforcements moving into the bridgehead.

The *Leibstandarte*'s commander, Theodor Wisch, was forward monitoring the battle from a hill just behind the panzer kampfgruppe. He watched as a group of T-34s managed to break free from the battle with the *Totenkopf* and swing right into the *Leibstandarte*'s flank held by its reconnaissance unit. A handful of Russian tanks managed to get past the reconnaissance battalion's antitank guns, and charged forward into the division's rear area, shooting up trucks and small groups of Waffen-SS men until they were put out of action by the *Leibstandarte*'s artillery regiment firing its guns in the antitank mode.

By early afternoon the battle in front of Prokhorovka reached its climax, first with Russian infantry supported by tanks advancing directly out of the town towards the *Leibstandarte*'s panzergrenadiers. A panzer counterattack broke up the infantry formation, and 40 tanks were claimed destroyed at long range. An hour later, the panzer kampfgruppe was moved northeastwards to clear out the 100 or so Soviet tanks believed to be hiding in the Psel valley. The *Leibstandarte*'s three remaining Tigers were then placed at the front of the panzerkeil. The force had only moved a few hundred metres when directly ahead more than 100 T-34s could be seen charging towards the German formation. This was the last hurrah of Rotmistrov's XVIII Tank Corps, and would see the destruction of the whole of the 181st Tank Brigade.

At a range of 1800m (5905ft), the Tigers started to take a toll of the Russian tanks. One after another the T-34s exploded in huge fireballs. Still the Russians kept coming. At 1000m (3280ft), every shot from the Tigers' 88mm cannons were scoring hits. Up to 10 tanks a minute were being hit as the Soviet brigade continued to surge forward. The Russians tried to return fire, but they were firing on the move, and few of them were able to hit any of the German tanks. Now the famous incident occurred when a T-34 tried to ram the Tiger of the famous *Leibstandarte* tank commander, SS-Untersturmführer Michael Wittmann, at high

KURSK

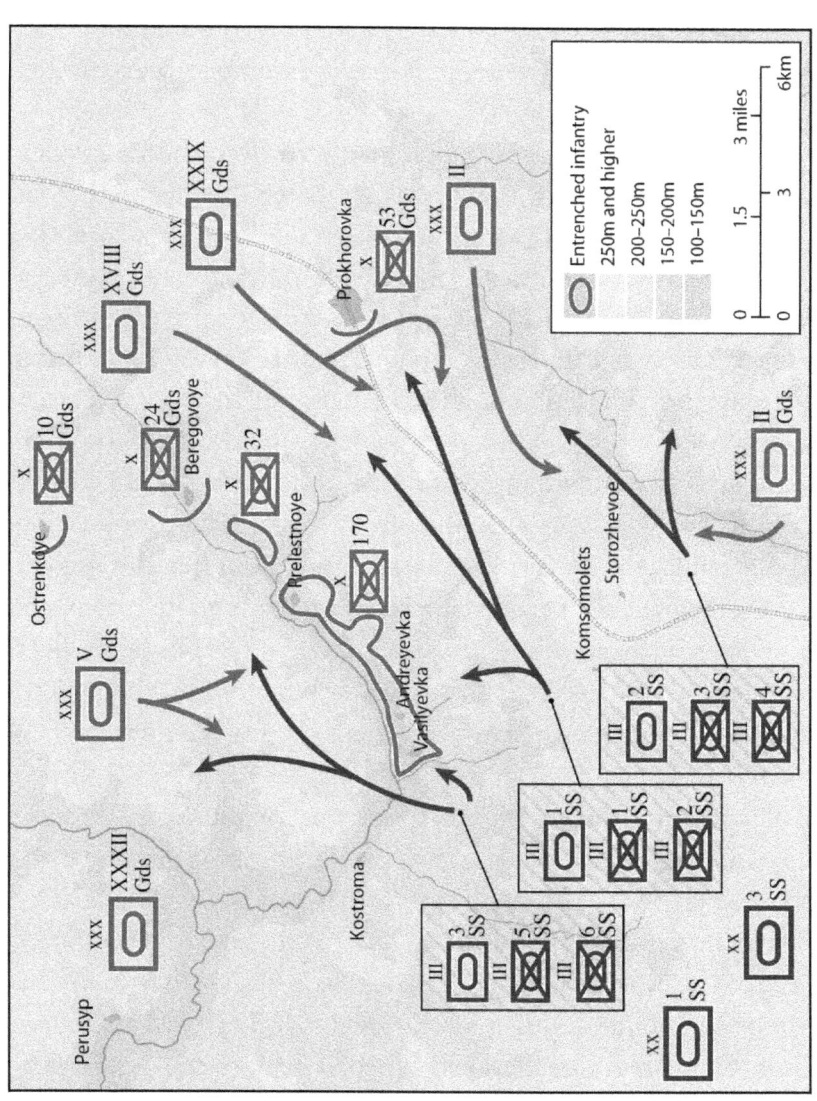

The Battle of Kursk: Prokhorovka 12 July 1943

speed. The Tiger survived the impact and was able to back-off from the wrecked Russian tank before its ammunition exploded. The 181st Tank Brigade failed to penetrate the German line, and for much of the afternoon the *Leibstandarte*'s panzers hunted down its remnants along the northern edge of the battlefield.

A tank brigade tried to launch an attack from the Psel valley later in the afternoon, but its T-34s barely got forward from their assembly area before accurate German 88mm fire from the Tigers broke up the attack. In the Psel valley the remnants of several Soviet tank brigades and battalions were trying to sort themselves out after being rebuffed with heavy losses during the day's battles. Commanders were trying to muster scratch battalions from the survivors, in order to rejoin the fight. Two more attacks were attempted towards the end of the afternoon, only to get the same reception from the German tanks. The Soviet tank crews were now starting to show a healthy respect for the Waffen-SS panzers, and made few attempts to emerge from cover. In addition, the *Leibstandarte* Division's artillery regiment now started to direct regular barrages into the area to make sure that the Russian troops kept their heads down.

On the *Das Reich*'s front the battle was equally fierce, with two tank corps and several infantry divisions trying to batter through its position from late in the morning. The brunt of these attacks were borne by the division's two panzergrenadier regiments, *Der Führer* in the south and *Deutschland* to the immediate right of *Leibstandarte*, which set up a series of defensive fronts in the woods and gullies south of Prokhorovka. II Tank and II Guards Tank Corps had already been blooded against the Waffen-SS over the previous week, and were now far more cautious in exposing their tanks to German firepower.

KURSK

A series of coordinated brigade-sized infantry and armour attacks were launched throughout the day, beginning at 11:40 hours with a push against *Der Führer*'s second battalion led by 30 T-34s. At the same time, an infantry attack hit *Deutschland*'s front.

Barely had the *Das Reich* Division seen off these human-wave infantry assaults, when *Der Führer* was bounced by a two-pronged attack. The regiment's front was engulfed by thousands of Russian infantry charging forward at the Waffen-SS lines. One German battalion also counted 40 Russian tanks advancing towards its lines among the infantry. In the north of the regiment's sector, another 70 tanks tried to push through to the Belgorod–Prokhorovka railway line at 14:00 hours.

Waffen-SS assault guns and antitank guns were pushed forward to repulse the Russian attacks, which went on well into the afternoon. At 15:00 hours, *Das Reich*'s panzer kampfgruppe was mustered from its reserve positions to counterattack and neutralize the Soviet threat once and for all. Two Soviet tank brigades were decimated in the sweep and 21 T-34s destroyed. This calmed the situation for a few hours. The Soviets were not finished yet, though, and they pushed forward again at 17:00 hours to try to force a breach between *Das Reich* and the 167th Infantry Division. As nightfall approached, the Soviet attack on *Das Reich* had well and truly run out of steam.

Over on the western flank of the battlefield, the *Totenkopf* Division was still battling to break out of its bridgehead. As the pressure mounted on German defences in front of Prokhorovka during the morning, the division was ordered to swing a kampfgruppe back across the Psel to strike into the Soviet armour using the valley as a base to attack the *Leibstandarte* Division. This attack made some progress and kept the Soviets bottled up in their "valley of death" for the rest of the day. The *schwerpunkt* of the division's efforts was to the north, and at 12:30 hours its panzer kampfgruppe was launched northwards through a huge barrage of Katyusha rocket fire. The *Totenkopf*'s panzers, with their 10 Tiger tanks in the lead, swept all before them. Its advance rolled 3.2km (two miles) north to cut the main road north out of Prokhorovka, and only the onset of darkness brought it to a halt. The division's panzers claimed the destruction of 27 Russian tanks in the advance. Follow-up panzergrenadiers made slower progress in the face of determined Soviet infantry, who fought to the last in the villages and woods around the bridgehead. This meant only a narrow corridor could be kept open from the bridgehead to the panzer spearhead to the north. Soviet counterattacks and artillery barrages rained down on the *Totenkopf* Division well into the night, inflicting heavy casualties. The division's panzers suffered heavily, with more than 45 out of 94 being put out of action, including all of its Tigers. Heavy rain showers washed the battlefield during the early evening, extinguishing many of the 400 burning tank hulks that were arrayed in front of the German lines. In the rain, repair crews from both sides tried to recover the remains of the damaged tanks to patch them up for next day's combat.

A string of top Soviet generals visited the battlefield to congratulate Rotmistrov on his great "victory". He had stopped the elite of Hitler's hated SS in their tracks and still held Prokhorovka. When Rotmistrov toured his shattered command to see for himself if it could be made ready for action the following day, he could be forgiven for thinking he had suffered a massive defeat. XXIX Tank Corps had lost 60 percent of its tanks and XVIII Tank Corps had suffered 30 percent losses. On 13 July, Rotmistrov admitted that his tank army could only field 100 to 150 combat-ready tanks out of the 850 committed for action at Prokhorovka on the previous day. The remainder had been destroyed or were too badly damaged to be considered fit for action.

Controversy has surrounded German tank losses in this crucial battle, with Rotmistrov and other Soviet histories claiming the Waffen-SS lost more than 300 tanks, including 70 Tiger tanks, during the action in front of Prokhorovka during 12 July. German records, however, paint a different picture. The Germans admitted to losing 70 to 80 tanks on that day, the majority of which were lost by the *Totenkopf* Division. The *Das Reich's* mechanics had already repaired scores of tanks damaged earlier in the offensive, so that on the morning of 13 July they actually had more tanks available than on the day before; while the *Leibstandarte* Division was only some 17 tanks down on the previous day's total.

When Hausser saw the tank kill claims coming from the battlefield, he could scarcely believe his eyes. The *Leibstandarte* Division alone claimed 192 Soviet tanks destroyed. The Waffen-SS general thought this was scarcely credible until he visited the battlefield and walked around the hulks, numbering them with chalk to avoid double-counting and confirm the kills accurately. Rotmistrov's own admissions of his tank losses tally in many ways with German figures, indicating that his tank charge, when considered on its own, might be classed as one of the most disastrous actions in military history.

After a night of rest, the battle resumed with a desultory infantry battle along the whole of the battle front. The Russians now started to push their infantry forward in major attacks, backed by heavy artillery fire, to compensate for their enormous tank losses. The *Leibstandarte*'s panzers and reconnaissance troops pushed forward to probe the strength of the Russian defences. Heavy antitank fire met the German patrols, and they withdrew back to their lines.

The *Totenkopf* Division was the main target of the Soviet effort. The division's understrength panzer kampfgruppe acted as a fire brigade inside the Psel bridgehead, moving to threatened sectors to stamp out Russian breakthroughs. The Red Air Force was now making its presence felt over the battlefield in strength, and the *Totenkopf*'s flak gunners were much in demand to protect the division from Stormovik fighter-bombers. Soviet tank losses continued to mount along the Psel front, with 38 T-34s alone being destroyed by the *Totenkopf*'s antitank battalion during one 20-minute incursion.

The offensive strength of II Waffen-SS Panzer Corps now rested in the *Das Reich* Division, and it pushed forward to attempt to link up with III Panzer Corps that was pushing northwards from east of Belgorod. *Das Reich*'s Tiger company spearheaded the advance that brushed aside several Russian tank counterattacks on 13 and 14 July, destroying at least eight T-34s. The advance continued for two more days, with village after village having to be cleared of Soviet defenders. On the morning of 15 July, it linked up with the 7th Panzer Division to close the ring around several thousand Red Army soldiers of XXXXVIII Rifle Corps and II Guards Tank Corps. An attempt to push northwards to outflank Prokhorovka from the east ran into heavy defences. As

KURSK

the *Das Reich* battled forward, the *Leibstandarte* and *Totenkopf* Divisions set about rebuilding their strength for another push northwards to finish off the Fifth Guards Tank Army for good. They were not to get the opportunity.

On 13 July, Hitler summoned his Eastern Front commanders to his East Prussian headquarters to issue new orders. Three days before, British and American troops had landed in Sicily, and the Ninth Army on the northern shoulder of the Kursk salient had been hit by a massive Soviet offensive that sent it reeling backwards in confusion. Hitler wanted to strip the Eastern Front of troops to shore up the Mediterranean.

Manstein pleaded to be allowed to continue his offensive to smash the last Soviet armoured reserves along the southern shoulder of the salient. Hitler agreed to this limited objective, but his attention was now focused on ensuring that the Italians were not knocked out of the war by further allied moves in the Mediterranean. XXIV Panzer Corps was not to be committed to exploit any success that II SS Panzer Corps might achieve. The final nails in the coffin of Operation Citadel were new Soviet offensives on 17 July, far to the south along the River Mius Front and at Izyum, which threatened the German hold on the strategically important southern Ukraine. These operations were deliberate deception, or *maskirovka*, moves, timed to distract German armour from the Kursk Front, which was entering a critical phase with Soviet tank reserves all but exhausted. Hitler fell for the ruse, ordering that II SS Panzer Corps be pulled out of the battle for the Kursk salient and sent southwards to neutralize this new threat. Operation Citadel was officially over.

The *Totenkopf*'s bridgehead over the Psel represented the high watermark of the Third Reich. Manstein and former Waffen-

SS generals later claimed that if the Führer had held his nerve for a few more days, victory would have been achieved. The Waffen-SS claimed a huge number of tank kills – 1149 in total – during Operation Citadel, along with the destruction of 459 antitank guns, 85 aircraft and 47 artillery pieces. Hausser's men also took 6441 prisoners. This, indeed, could be considered a great tactical victory. However, from the Soviet viewpoint the battle was a strategic success. Their defence tactics worked, preventing the Germans breaking through into the open and using their Blitzkrieg-style of warfare to outflank, confuse and surround the Russians. The cost in lives and tanks was huge, but the Germans were never able to create a decisive breakthrough. Hitler would not give his commanders the time they needed to punch through to Kursk.

Fires were breaking out all along the borders of the Third Reich. Hitler insisted on rushing Waffen-SS panzer divisions to wherever a crisis loomed. They had become the Führer's "Fire Brigade". The Soviet High Command, however, fully understood Germany's many weaknesses and devised a strategy to defeat them. They held out at Prokhorovka – only just – and immediately applied pressure elsewhere to force the Germans to pull out their steadily dwindling panzer divisions to plug the holes. The Waffen-SS panzers may have been masters of the battlefield at Prokhorovka, but the Soviets were now masters of strategy on the Eastern Front. From now on the Wehrmacht would dance to the Red Army's tune.

The carefully gathered panzer reserves had been largely spent, while the Red Army, though perhaps suffering up to 250,000 casualties at Kursk, was now free to launch its own strategic offensive on the Eastern Front. As Manstein stated: "Henceforth

KURSK

Southern Army Group found itself waging a defensive struggle which could not be anything more than a system of improvisations and stop-gaps. Being too weak, on that widely extended front, for purely passive defence against an enemy so many times stronger than itself, it had to concentrate its efforts – even at the risk of repercussions in sectors temporarily less threatened – on punctually assembling forces whenever there was a Soviet breakthrough to intercept or a chance of inflicting a blow on the enemy. What had to be avoided at all costs was that any elements of the Army Group should become cut off through deep enemy breakthroughs and suffer the same fate as Sixth Army at Stalingrad. To 'maintain ourselves in the field', and in doing so wear down the enemy's offensive capacity to the utmost, became the whole essence of this struggle."

And during the final period of the war on the Eastern Front, up to the very end of the Third Reich, the Waffen-SS panzer divisions would be called upon again and again by a desperate Führer to save seemingly impossible situations.

Chapter 5

DEATH RIDE OF THE *TOTENKOPF*

The Waffen-SS is bled white on the Mius Front, July 1943.

Barely two weeks after the end of Operation Citadel (see Chapter 4), II SS Panzer Corps was thrown into a new battle. In three days of fighting along the River Mius Front, in the southern Ukraine, Adolf Hitler's elite Waffen-SS panzer divisions would suffer more casualties than during the two-week swirling tank battles south of Kursk. Thrown into a bloody frontal assault, the *Totenkopf* and *Das Reich* Divisions suffered thousands of casualties from dug-in Soviet antitank guns and machine-gun nests. The Waffen-SS divisions eventually drove the Soviets from their bridge head across the Mius, but the Führer's "Fire Brigade" lost irreplaceable men and equipment at a crucial time when the fate of the Eastern Front hung in the balance.

It took the Waffen-SS only a few days to disengage from the Prokhorovka region after Adolf Hitler cancelled Operation Citadel on 17 July 1943. Plans were now prepared for counteroffensives to destroy the Soviet bridgeheads across the Mius and the Donets at Izyum. The *Leibstandarte* and *Das Reich* Divisions, with the 17th Panzer Division and 333rd Infantry Division in support, were to crush the Izyum incursion with an assault beginning on 24 July. This was to be a quick containment operation, lasting only a few days, to allow II SS Panzer Corps to be free to deal with the Mius Front.

No sooner had the Waffen-SS troops been deployed in their attack positions than the order arrived from the Führer's headquarters cancelling the operation. He had other work for them. The *Leibstandarte* was loaded onto trains, minus its tanks which were to be handed over to the *Das Reich* and *Totenkopf* Divisions, and sent westwards to help shore up Mussolini's fascist regime in Italy after the Allied invasion of Sicily in early July 1943. The Izyum counterattack would be left to the elite Waffen-SS *Wiking* Division and the 17th Panzer Division. In two weeks of bitter fighting the two formations contained the Soviet bridgehead, but did not have the strength to actually wipe it out.

The remaining units of II SS Panzer Corps were now loaded on to trains again and sent off to the Mius Front, where a far more serious crisis was developing that threatened to break open the southern front of Field Marshal von Manstein's Army Group South. For the Waffen-SS men this was a confusing time – they received little information apart from the time their trains were leaving to various "destinations unknown". Once they arrived they were expected to be ready for action in a few hours.

The last 160km (100 miles) of the River Mius flow almost exactly along a north–south course into the Gulf of Taganrog. The German "new" Sixth Army had been defending this line since the spring, with 10 understrength infantry divisions and a single weak panzergrenadier division. The Mius was the last natural obstacle before the great River Dnieper, and Hitler believed it was the key to protecting the Ukraine's natural resources and industrial potential from the Red Army.

In mid-July 1943 the river was reduced to barely a trickle. It was only some 50m (164ft) wide and a few centimetres deep. The Sixth Army had spent almost six months building up its defences on the high ground on the western bank, but the 12.8km- (eight-mile-) long slope up from the river meant the German positions were dangerously exposed to Russian observation and artillery fire. The high ground was featureless, with only a handful of small villages and ravines providing any protection from artillery fire. However, huge wheat fields with nearly ripe crops covered the slopes, making it very easy for infantrymen to disappear from view. Along the river bank there was little cover, and the only way for the Germans to protect themselves was to dig deep trench lines and bunkers. They also planted numerous minefields to channel any attacks into killing zones. In the run-up to Operation Citadel, the Mius Front was a backwater, with few reinforcement troops and tanks being sent to help bolster the Sixth Army. It had much in common with the fictional section of the Eastern Front portrayed in the 1977 Sam Pekinpah movie, Cross of Iron.

DEATH RIDE OF THE TOTENKOPF

The Soviet High Command had great plans for the Mius Front. They saw it as a key pressure point to draw away the German panzer reserves if their front around Kursk was ever seriously threatened. In a classic campaign of maskirovka, or deception, they carried out all the preparations for their Mius offensive in full view of the Germans. Tank and truck convoys moved into position at night with headlights on. Radio conversations detailing attack plans were made with no attempt to encode secret information. Artillery positions were set up in the open and stockpiles of ammunition were not hidden. As the giant tank battle at Prokhorovka reached its climax, the Soviets ordered their troops on the Mius to attack. There were tank reserves on hand to exploit any breakthrough, but the incursion would, hopefully, panic the Germans into moving panzers away from the decisive front. Tens of thousands of Red Army soldiers would die in the coming weeks to satisfy the Soviet master deception plan.

The opening attack on 17 July went like clockwork for the Soviets. Several small-scale attacks on the northern and southern wings of the Mius line were easily repulsed. In the centre of the front, between the towns of Kuibyshevo and Dmitrievka, the Russians threw their II Guards Mechanized Corps into action, with 120 T-34 and 80 T-70 tanks in the first assault wave. They smashed through the German first line with ease. Although briefly delayed by German minefields and infantry counterattacks, the Soviet advance seemed unstoppable. The commander of the Sixth Army, Infantry General Karl Hollidt, threw in his only reserve, the 16th Panzergrenadier Division, with its 40 or so tanks, on 18 July. The division was given little time to prepare or plan the operation, and it was a total disaster.

Overnight, the Soviets had brought up scores of antitank guns and the German division's panzer battalion had barely crossed its start line when it ran into a hailstorm of fire. In the space of a few minutes it lost more than 20 tanks, and had to pull back in disorder. The Soviets pressed forward to exploit their advantage, seizing the summits of the ridges high above the River Mius.

Manstein now sent Hollidt the 23rd Panzer Division to give him more armour to turn back the Soviet tide. However, its attack on 19 July was just as disastrous as the efforts of the 16th Panzergrenadier Division, losing 28 of its 50 tanks in a direct frontal attack on the Russian line. Again the Soviets pressed home their advantage, with a major attack by IV Mechanized Corps being mounted on 22 July. Its 140 tanks rolled forward to take on the Sixth Army's remaining 36 panzers. Only the arrival of XXIV Panzer Corps headquarters units saved the day. It organized a rapid improvised defensive line of 88mm flak guns and Sturmgeschütz (StuG) III assault gun batteries to repel the Soviet tank armada. Now it was the Germans' turn to inflict havoc on the Soviets. The 88mm flak gunners used their powerful weapons to great effect, picking off 93 Soviet tanks and breaking the back of the enemy attack. With its last reserves of tanks shattered, the Red Army offensive ran out of steam. It was now the turn of the Germans to attack.

After its diversion to the Izyum Front, II SS Panzer Corps was not available to lead the Mius counterstroke until 29 July. The *Totenkopf* Division, led by SS-Brigadeführer Hermann Priess, arrived on the Mius Front first, followed by elements of *Das Reich*. Hollidt was a firm believer in the principle of launching immediate counterattacks to dislodge any Soviet incursions to prevent the enemy fortifying their positions. In the past, rapid counterattacks had always driven the Soviets back in confusion. His experience with the 16th Panzergrenadier and 23rd Panzer Divisions did nothing to lead Hollidt to change his mind. II SS Panzer Corps would therefore be sent straight into action, with no time to familiarize itself with the ground or scout out the enemy's weak points. Hollidt was not interested in a deep flanking attack to trap the whole Russian attack force in a massive pocket. He wanted a frontal assault, and he wanted it on 30 July. Never ones to miss a chance to prove that they could do what the army had failed to accomplish, the Waffen-SS commanders went about their new mission with gusto.

The *Totenkopf*'s objective was a ridge line in the centre of the Russian position. A complete Soviet antitank brigade with scores of 76.2mm high-velocity antitank guns, supported by dug-in T-34s and elements of five infantry divisions, had had five days to turn the Waffen-SS division's objective into a fortress. Immediately to the south, *Das Reich's Deutschland* Panzergrenadier Regiment was to assault the heavily fortified town of Stepanovka, to seize a nearby hill which was the highest point in the Mius region. The Soviet defenders knew their trade, though, and they had created a mutually supporting network of pak-fronts, so any German tanks that tried to attack one antitank battery could be hit in the flank by accurate fire from another battery.

The *Totenkopf*'s attack was to be spearheaded by SS Panzer Regiment 3, with its 49 Panzer IIIs, nine Panzer IVs and 10 Tiger Is. The division's two panzergrenadier regiments, *Theodor Eicke* and *Totenkopf*, followed behind in echelon to clear out Soviet infantry positions. As usual, the Tigers were positioned at the front of the *Totenkopf* panzerkeil.

As the attack rolled forward just after dawn on 30 July, everything seemed be going well until the panzers moved into range of the pak-fronts. A furious barrage of accurate heavy antitank rounds started to rain down on the German tanks. Russian infantry then joined in, with their antitank rifles aimed at the panzers' thinner side armour. To compound the problem, heavy artillery started to land among the attack formation, forcing the panzergrenadiers to run for shelter.

The Russian fire forced the panzers to try to take cover in ravines or folds in the ground. Each tank was now taking multiple hits, and it was difficult to find any cover from the fire, which was coming in from both the front and side. Whole Soviet antitank batteries were concentrating their fire on individual German tanks, until they either pulled back or were knocked out. Even the heavily armoured Tigers found they could not survive this ordeal. As if things were not bad enough, suddenly the *Totenkopf*'s tank crews found they had blundered into a minefield. Tank after tank had its tracks blown off, and the immobilized panzers were easily picked off one by one by Soviet gunners. In less than two hours the attack had all but ground to a halt, with some 48 tanks, including eight Tiger Is, and scores of other light armoured vehicles being put out of action.

It was now up to the panzergrenadiers to take the lead. Combat engineers came forward under heavy Soviet machine-gun and mortar fire to clear assault lanes through the minefields. Artillery and rocket fire was brought down on the Soviet line to cover the advance, but the fire support broke down when one of the Nebelwerfer launchers exploded, throwing the German fire base into confusion. Now Soviet

Stormovik fighter-bombers appeared over the battlefield in large numbers to strafe the Waffen-SS attack troops. By the middle of the day, the Soviet defence was holding and the battlefield was obscured by the smoke from dozens of burning German tanks. A rare Stuka dive-bomber attack in the early afternoon allowed the *Totenkopf* Regiment's combat engineers to clear two lanes through the minefield. Some of the few remaining panzers were brought up to support the panzergrenadier attack. The attack force inched from one ravine to the next, with the tanks providing fire support for the infantry assaults. The Russians staged a counterattack with half a dozen T-34s, but it was quickly beaten back by the Panzers – a rare success for the Waffen-SS. By the time it started to get dark, the *Totenkopf* Division had made no serious impression on the main Soviet defence line. Its panzer regiment had lost almost all of its tanks, although many would be repaired over the coming days, and just under 500 men had been either killed or wounded. The division's panzergrenadier companies were devastated, some losing more than 60 combat soldiers out of an original strength of 90 men.

The *Das Reich* Division's attack on Stepanovka was equally unsuccessful. It had two kampfgruppen available for action, because most of the *Der Führer* Panzergrenadier Regiment was stuck on muddy roads far to the north. The *Deutschland* Panzergrenadier Regiment was to storm into Stepanovka, backed by the division's assault gun battalion. Panzer Regiment 2, the reconnaissance battalion and the armoured personnel carrier battalion of the *Der Führer* Regiment would make a sweep to the south of the village, to take the key hill that dominated the whole region.

Preceded by a snap artillery barrage from *Das Reich*'s self-propelled artillery battery, the *Deutschland* Regiment successfully charged into the town, but then its problems began. The Soviets had fortified every building and the Waffen-SS men soon found themselves fighting for their lives. Mines, booby traps and snipers were waiting for them in large numbers. The attackers barely managed to push into the town deeper than a few streets. Roving T-34s patrolled the town's streets, blasting any Germans who tried to move in the open. *Das Reich*'s panzer kampfgruppe fared slightly better than the *Totenkopf*'s tanks, though. In spite of losing 25 tanks in minefields, it was able to capture two hill-top strongpoints before its attack soon bogged down.

German casualties in Stepanovka were mounting at an alarming rate, with many companies now commanded by junior lieutenants or senior noncommissioned officers due to losses among senior officers. Not even the deployment of the reconnaissance battalion's 20mm flak guns in the direct fire role was able to dislodge the Soviet defenders from their bunkers and tunnels. By the end of the day, *Das Reich* had lost more than 320 casualties for little gain.

The *Totenkopf*'s commander, Priess, was determined to press ahead with the assault and decided that more guile was needed to winkle the Soviets out from their defensive positions. He ordered his panzergrenadiers to launch a surprise "silent" night assault to clear out the Soviet defences. While the initial assault got into the Russian trenches undetected, the Soviets reacted quickly and drove the Germans back with a very prompt counterattack. The incident, however, distracted the Russians long enough for *Totenkopf*'s combat engineers to clear more than 2000 mines and create new lanes through the minefields.

Battle for Stepanovka

The Waffen-SS attack on 31 July was far better planned, with a 45-minute artillery fire preparation by all of II SS Panzer Corps' artillery and rocket launchers. Stuka dive-bombers were on call in strength for the first time in the operation. This time, also, a huge rolling barrage was employed to shield the remaining *Totenkopf* panzers and supporting infantry as they moved forward. The attack breached the first Soviet defence line but it soon stalled. Again

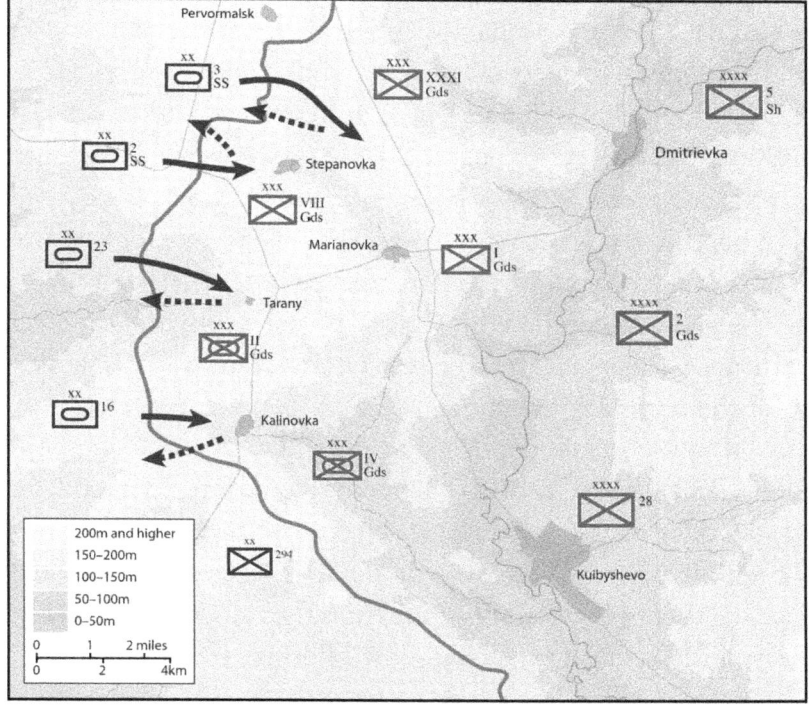

The Mius Bridgehead: 30 July 1943

casualties were horrendous, with one Waffen-SS assault battalion reduced to less than 100 men. The division was now reduced to one Tiger, nine Panzer IVs and five Panzer III tanks.

In the *Das Reich* Division's sector, the Russians launched no less than 14 counterattacks, backed by more than 70 tanks, as they tried to turf the Waffen-SS out of Stepanovka. Fighting during the afternoon was halted by a torrential downpour that turned the battlefield into a quagmire. The storm at one point put the *Totenkopf*'s divisional headquarters out of action, when a violent flash-flood surged down the ravine it was positioned in, washing away radio antennae and command trucks and creating all round general disorder.

The day's action was hardly encouraging for the Waffen-SS, with another 400 men killed or wounded and 24 more tanks destroyed. Another 80 tanks were in workshops under repair. If this rate of losses continued, II SS Panzer Corps would cease to exist as an effective fighting force. Manstein was so concerned that his elite armoured reserve was being bled white for no gain, that he visited Hollidt's headquarters to order the offensive to be called off. He needed the Waffen-SS panzer divisions to deal with an anticipated Soviet offensive at Kharkov, and did not want them to suffer any more losses.

In a tense conference during 31 July, SS-Obergruppenführer Paul Hausser insisted that his men could finish the job. The commander of the *Der Führer* Regiment, SS-Obersturmbannführer Silvester Stadler, was produced to convince the field marshal that his fresh troops could turn the tide. His enthusiasm swayed Manstein into allowing the offensive to continue for a "few more days". Radical new tactics were now to be employed to prevent a repeat of the past two days' slaughter.

DEATH RIDE OF THE TOTENKOPF

Stadler was allowed to spend the rest of the day making a thorough reconnaissance of the sector south of Stepanovka. At 04:00 hours on 1 August, the two unblooded battalions were launched forward to seize the high ground below the town, with *Das Reich*'s panzer kampfgruppe in support.

Firestorm of firepower
Simultaneously, 600 German guns and Nebelwerfers launched a massive barrage along the entire length of the Russian frontline. Hundreds of antitank gun pits and infantry bunkers, that had been pinpointed during the previous two days' battles, were targeted during the barrage. In the sector to be assaulted by Stadler's troops, the Nebelwerfers laid a huge smokescreen to cover their dash across open ground. The tactics worked, and within a few minutes the Waffen-SS men were over the enemy's barbed wire, throwing grenades into their trenches and bunkers. A couple of hours of fierce hand-to-hand fighting followed as Stadler and his men swept into the Russian strong-point. Defeated, the Soviet infantry retreated down the hill, leaving Stadler with control of the summit. He barely had time to admire the superb view of the battlefield, though, when a massive Soviet artillery fire mission landed on the position, forcing his panzergrenadiers to take cover in the old Russian trenches. Stadler's small command team now dived under an abandoned T-34 tank. Disaster then struck, when a Soviet shell destroyed all his radios. German artillery observers on nearby hills had no idea that the Waffen-SS had taken the hill, and decided to join in the battle, blasting the strong-point with their own fire. Only the firing of a signal flare brought this madness to an end. Now a human-wave attack by Soviet infantry, backed by T-34s, started to move up

the hill. By some miracle, Stadler's command team were able to get a radio working and started to call down artillery fire on the advancing enemy. This fire, combined with *Der Führer* Regiment's own MG 42 machine-gun fire, left a pile of corpses along the hill's southern slope. A few assault guns now appeared, and they knocked out the Russian tanks that had survived the carnage and pressed home their attack. A repeat performance a few minutes later received similar treatment from Stadler's men, who were now firmly established in their new positions.

In parallel with Stadler's attack, *Das Reich*'s panzer kampfgruppe attacked eastwards to bypass Stepanovka and push through to take the Soviet antitank guns holding up the *Totenkopf* Division in the flank. Heavy antitank gun fire halted the panzers south of Stepanovka as they moved forward. The panzergrenadiers dismounted from their armoured personnel carriers and assaulted the small pak-front blocking the way forward. Stukas were called in to blast a hole in the Soviet defence line, opening the way for the panzers. The job of leading the advance now fell to a Waffen-SS assault gun battery. Its StuG IIIs swept all before them, and were soon raking the Soviet antitank brigade's positions blocking the *Totenkopf* from the rear. The latter was at last able to move forward. Its panzergrenadiers sealed the ring around Stepanovka during the afternoon, allowing the *Deutschland* Regiment to clear the town of its last defenders.

Farther to the north, the *Totenkopf*'s remaining 19 panzers were at last moving forward. The morning's massive artillery preparation and the success of the *Das Reich*'s attacks significantly reduced the weight of fire that the Soviet defenders could lay down. Stuka attacks neutralized many pockets of resistance, and the Nebelwerfers were used to screen the German tanks from antitank gun fire.

By 16:00 hours, the main Russian strong-point blocking the SS advance was cleared. A massive Soviet counterattack now materialized. Several regiments of Russian infantry surged up the hill in a series of assaults. The few remaining German tanks turned their machine guns on the mass of brown uniforms that were covering the hillside. The intervention of the Luftwaffe was decisive, when a wave of Stukas dived on the Russian attack group. The low-level bombing and strafing broke the back of the attack, and hundreds of Russians started to surrender. Thousands more fled back towards the bridges over the Mius. For the men of the *Totenkopf* Division, the air strike could not have come a moment too soon. Only a few hundred German troops were inside the captured strong-point, and they would have had no chance of survival if the Russians had reached them.

From their vantage points, the Waffen-SS assault troops could see huge Russian convoys moving across the Mius bridges. The Red Army was retreating from its bridgehead.

II SS Panzer Corps spent another day on the Mius Front, helping the Sixth Army mop up the last pockets of Russian resistance on the west bank of the river. It had already received new orders to pull out of the Mius Front and move northwards to counter a fresh Soviet offensive around Kharkov that was growing into a major threat. Only the *Totenkopf* and *Das Reich* Divisions would be committed to this new battle. Hitler wanted Hausser's headquarters to immediately move to northern Italy, to shore-up his forces being mustered to repel the imminent Allied invasion of the Italian mainland.

As the *Totenkopf* and *Das Reich* Divisions started to pull in their scattered units ready for loading onto trains for the move northwards, the scale of the bloodbath on the Mius became apparent In three days of battle, the *Totenkopf* Division lost 1500 dead and wounded. This was three times the number of its casualties during Operation Citadel. Crucially, most of the losses were among the division's combat regiments, particularly the panzer regiment and panzergrenadiers. The losses in junior officers and company level commanders were grievous indeed. The Waffen-SS ethos of leadership from the front was proving to be very costly. *Das Reich*'s losses were nearly as bad, bringing its total dead and wounded during the previous month up to 2811. The two divisions would be thrown into battle again during the next week without time to recover from their losses, and no replacements would arrive for many more weeks (the army was also suffering from lack of replacements: at this time Manstein's 38 infantry divisions in Army Group South had a fighting strength of only 18, and his 14 panzer divisions of only six).

The two divisions' tank losses were horrendous, with the *Totenkopf* only being able to muster 23 tanks fit for action on 2 August 1943. *Das Reich*, likewise, could only field 22 tanks. Both divisions also had approximately a dozen assault guns and a similar number of Marder self-propelled antitank guns. Prior to the Mius operation, the combined II SS Panzer Corps armoured strength had been some 190 tanks and assault guns. While many of the damaged Waffen-SS tanks and assault guns were soon back in action following rapid repairs, the scale of the slaughter inflicted by the Russian defences along the Mius was unprecedented.

DEATH RIDE OF THE TOTENKOPF

Although German commanders tried to portray the Mius operation as a great success because of the 18,000 prisoners taken and 585 Soviet tanks knocked out, the battle was only a Pyrrhic victory. Stalin's generals had successfully drawn Manstein's precious panzer reserves into battle in a backwater on the Eastern Front, and had bled them white.

Chapter 6
THE FUHRER'S FIRE BRIGADE

The withdrawal from Kharkov and the retreat to the Dnieper.

While the bloody battles raged along the River Mius Front, the Soviet High Command used the breathing space caused by the departure of the Waffen-SS panzer divisions in the northeastern Ukraine to prepare for the decisive offensive to break the German hold on the Eastern Front once and for all. The Soviet First Tank Army, Sixth Guards Army and Fifth Guards Tank Army, which had escaped the German *coup de grâce* at Prokhorovka by Adolf Hitler's decision to prematurely call off Operation Citadel, were quickly rebuilt for offensive operations. Men and resources were allocated to the units decimated at

Kursk to bring them up to strength for Operation Rumyanstev, as the Soviets codenamed their new offensive. The offensive was to break along an axis from Belgorod to Kharkov, and then fan out westwards to drive the German Army Group South back to the River Dnieper. To ensure the success of the operation, Stalin massed 650,000 men and 2300 tanks north of Belgorod. They faced a shell-shocked Fourth Panzer Army and Army Detachment *Kempf*, which had received no respite since the end of Operation Citadel. They mustered only around 200,000 men and less than 300 tanks between them. The army panzer divisions committed to Operation Citadel had suffered far heavier casualties than the Waffen-SS, and still had not received any replacement tanks or men. The average divisional panzer strength was below 50 operational tanks. In most sectors, the Soviets were able to achieve a local supremacy in tank strength of 12 to one.

Not surprisingly, therefore, when Operation Rumyanstev was unleashed on 3 August 1943 it achieved dramatic successes. The brunt of the Soviet assault fell to the west of Belgorod against the sectors of XXXXVIII Panzer Corps and LII Corps respectively. The 19th Panzer Division could only put 28 tanks into action against the main Soviet axis of attack. It took the Russians only a matter of hours to crack open the German defences, and once a breach developed their was no way to seal it. A torrent of T-34s was unleashed.

The German XI Corps fought a dogged rearguard action along the Donets above Belgorod, and then pulled back in good order to Kharkov, repulsing repeated attempts to outflank its front. The 6th Panzer Division, 503rd Heavy Panzer Battalion with Tiger I tanks, and numerous independent assault gun battalions saved the day on numerous occasions as XI Corps fell back southwards.

In XXXXVIII Panzer Corps' sector chaos reigned. The commanders of both the corps and the 19th Panzer Division were killed in the confusion when their staff cars were ambushed by Soviet tanks. The isolated divisions of the corps fought desperate rearguard actions as they tried to retreat to safety in the south. A huge gap more than 32km (20 miles) wide had been torn in the German front, and the Soviet First Tank Army was advancing southwards at breakneck speed to exploit this very favourable situation. The Fifth Guards Tank Army was following close behind, ready to swing eastwards and encircle Kharkov itself.

Field Marshal Erich von Manstein now started to muster his panzer strike force to seal the gap in the line and defeat the Soviet tank armies. III Panzer Corps under Lieutenant-General Hermann Breith was ordered to take charge of the operation to defeat the Soviet thrust. He was to have the *Totenkopf*, *Das Reich* and *Wiking* Divisions for the mission, as well as the 3rd Panzer Division. However, at this time all the Waffen-SS divisions were still en route by train from the Izyum and Mius Fronts. In the meantime, the 3rd Panzer Division would have to hold the ring as best it could, and prevent Soviet tanks driving into Kharkov and capturing the de-training points of the Waffen-SS divisions.

Although it could only put 35 tanks in the field, the 3rd Panzer Division was a seasoned formation and it put up a good fight, staging a spirited rearguard action on 5 August against a push by the Soviet XVIII Tank Corps of the Fifth Guards Tank Army. The division repulsed this attack, and became a firm anchor on the right flank of III Panzer Corps.

Farther to the west, there was no German forces to stop the First Tank Army seizing the key rail junction at Bogodukhov on 6 August. Over the next two days the lead elements of the *Das Reich* Division started to arrive south of Kharkov, and they were fed piecemeal into the battle to try to shore up the front to the west of the city. Luftwaffe aerial reconnaissance was providing Breith with valuable photographs that showed thousands of Russians tanks moving southwards to the west of Kharkov. The Germans had never had to deal with an enemy offensive on this scale before.

By 8 August *Das Reich* was deployed in strength, with four Tigers and 20 assault guns in action. Even though its panzer regiment was still to arrive, the division was able to inflict heavy losses on the Soviet III Mechanized Corps and XXXI Tank Corps, which were spearheading the First Tank Army's advance. VI Tank Corps, however, was still advancing southwards unopposed.

It was now the turn of the *Totenkopf* Division to enter the battle, and try to close down the Soviet breakthrough. During the night of 8/9 August the division deployed across VI Tank Corps' axis of advance, ready to stop it in its tracks. The *Totenkopf* Panzergrenadier Regiment was to form the centre of the defence, with the reconnaissance battalion screening its left flank and the *Theodor Eicke* Panzergrenadier Regiment digging in on the right. In reserve was a company from SS Panzer Regiment 3 with 12 tanks. The remainder of the regiment's 14 Panzer IIIs and 27 Panzer IVs were still en route.

The Waffen-SS men had most of the morning to prepare their defences, before the storm broke. The Soviet 112th Tank Brigade charged at the front of a German-held village during the afternoon, with hundreds of "tommy gun"-armed infantry riding on the hulls of dozens of T-34 tanks. A furious battle raged in the streets of the village, at the centre of the *Totenkopf* Regiment's position, as small groups of Waffen-SS men destroyed the Soviet tanks with hollow-charge mines and machine-gun teams dealt with the tank-riding infantry. As this battle raged, two more Soviet tank brigades pushed west of the village, forcing the *Totenkopf*'s reconnaissance battalion back.

More German forces were arriving all the time, with the *Wiking* Division arriving to bolster the 3rd Panzer Division's front on the right flank of III Panzer Corps. It arrived just in time to meet an all-out offensive along the whole of the German corps' front on 10 August. In furious fighting, the 3rd Panzer and *Das Reich* Divisions held their lines, claiming 46 and 66 Soviet tanks destroyed respectively.

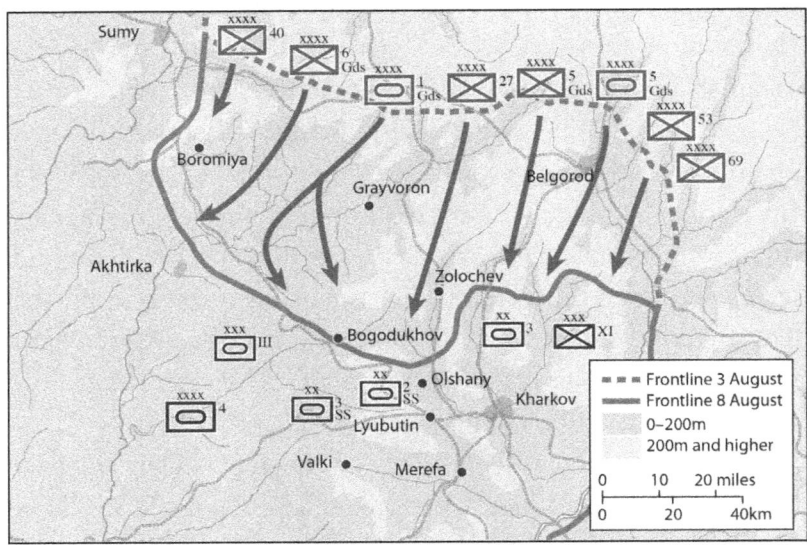

The Fourth Battle of Kharkov: 3–8 August 1943

THE FÜHRER'S FIRE BRIGADE

Although the *Totenkopf* held its front, three Soviet tank brigades swept past its left flank, pushing 16km (10 miles) forward. SS Panzer Regiment 3 now intervened in the battle to cut off the Soviet spearhead. In a desperate battle in vast cornfields, the Waffen-SS tanks sliced into the flank of the Soviet 1st Tank Brigade. Two panzer kampfgruppen fought throughout the day, knocking out scores of tanks and machine-gunning hundreds of Soviet troops. Individual *Totenkopf* tanks soon found themselves surrounded by swarms of Soviet tanks and infantry. The *Totenkopf*'s combat engineers joined the fight, setting up a blocking position ahead of the Soviet push. These interventions brought the Russian drive south to a halt – just. More disjointed and desperate fighting continued during 11 August, as the small *Totenkopf* units tried to establish a continuous front. The *Totenkopf*'s small Tiger detachment was particularly effective, destroying a Soviet infantry breakthrough.

The *Wiking* and *Das Reich* Divisions remained on the defensive, dealing with direct enemy frontal attacks across open corn fields by groups of 25–30 tanks and hundreds of infantry. Their panzers broke these attacks up with long-range fire.

The *Totenkopf* Panzer Regiment and combat engineers continued their desperate counterattack, driving back the Soviet 112th Tank Brigade, which lost 25 tanks and all of its antitank guns. This completed a strong defensive battle by the *Totenkopf* which accounted for 134 tanks of the 268 that the First Tank Army had started the day with.

With the First Tank Army taking heavy losses, the Soviet High Command ordered Marshal Pavel Rotmistrov's Fifth Guards Tank Army to swing in behind it and then take over the advance. XVIII and XXIX Tanks Corps took the lead on 12

August and pushed southwards, just as III Panzer Corps launched itself forward into what was left of the First Tank Army. Army Tiger tanks from the 503rd Heavy Tank Battalion joined the *Theodor Eicke* Regiment to slice into the flank of the First Tank Army, destroying scores of T-34s and forcing the 112th Tank Brigade to retreat northwards. *Totenkopf* panzers continued to clear out a group of VI Tank Corps troops cut off farther south, and also destroyed a relief column. The division's reconnaissance battalion set up another defensive line out to the west and, with the help of an 88mm flak gun detachment, drove off several attacks.

The *Theodor Eicke* Regiment's westward advance was now reinforced by the *Totenkopf* assault gun battalion, which knocked out 25 Soviet tanks that tried to press home a counterattack.

This advance was joined by the *Das Reich* Division, which was now attacking in a southwesterly direction. Its 22 panzers and 23 assault guns led a kampfgruppe formed around the *Der Führer* Panzergrenadier Regiment, which smashed into the lead tank brigade of the Fifth Guards Tank Army moving south to help its beleaguered comrades. The panzers turned back the first wave of unsuspecting Soviet tanks with ease. By the afternoon, though, the Russians had reorganized and launched a fresh attack in strength. XXXI Tank Corps then hit *Das Reich's* tanks and assault guns in a predictable display of tactical ineptitude. The Germans claimed the destruction of 70 Russian tanks and the death of the corps commander in the turret of his burning T-34. Many of these tanks belonged to XVIII Tank Corps, which had joined the battle late in the afternoon.

The *Wiking* Division also advanced during the day against a prepared Soviet defence line held by infantry units of the Soviet

THE FÜHRER'S FIRE BRIGADE

XXIX Tank Corps. SS Panzer Regiment 5 led the attack, but its 24 Panzer IIIs and 17 Panzer IVs could not punch through the strong Soviet antitank defence network. The day's swirling tank battles inflicted heavy losses on both sides, with the Soviets taking the largest share of the casualties. In five days of fighting the two Soviet tank armies had suffered grievous losses, with the First Tank Army now down to less than 150 operational tanks out of its original 500, and the Fifth Guards Tank Army down to 100 tanks out of a similar starting strength.

During the early hours of 13 August, the Russians again pressed forward regardless of losses. The fresh V Guards Tank Corps and 6th Motorized Brigade were used to batter their way past the *Totenkopf*'s reconnaissance battalion, and then push even farther south. III Panzer Corps' attack was now gathering momentum, though, as the *Totenkopf* and *Das Reich* Divisions pushed from east to west, with the aim of cutting off the Russian spearheads.

With Tiger tanks and assault guns in the lead, the Waffen-SS assault columns sliced through the shell-shocked elements of the First Tank Army that barred their way. Nebelwefer rocket barrages and Stuka dive-bombers were called in whenever resistance was encountered. The *Totenkopf*'s 88mm flak battery was in the vanguard of the advance to add to the firepower of the panzerkeil. All resistance was broken, and a series of futile counterattacks smashed as the advance moved relentlessly forward. *Das Reich* joined the attack with a vengeance, advancing close to the key rail junction at Bogodukhov. Scores of T-34s were knocked out to bring the combined "kill" total for the two Waffen-SS divisions in a 48-hour period to 200 tanks. *Wiking*'s panzergrenadiers also advanced, pushing back a Soviet infantry division guarding the western approach to the town.

As the *Totenkopf* advance gathered pace, its small panzer kampfgruppe stalked the shattered remnants of the Soviet tank brigades through sunflower fields. The Russians usually fled before the rampaging panzers. During the afternoon, a group of 30 T-34s tried to take on the panzers head-on. In a brief engagement the German Tigers and Panzer IVs formed a firing line, while the *Totenkopf*'s Panzer IIIs manoeuvred against the enemy's vulnerable flanks. The Soviets didn't realize the danger they were in and charged straight into the killing zone. None of the T-34s escaped the battle.

The flow of battle remained unchanged the next day, with more German successes as they pushed farther westwards, cutting across the supply lines of four Soviet infantry divisions and two tanks corps. Over the next two days the *Totenkopf* and *Das Reich* Divisions completed the encirclement of the 52nd and 90th Rifle Divisions, along with the remnants of V Guards

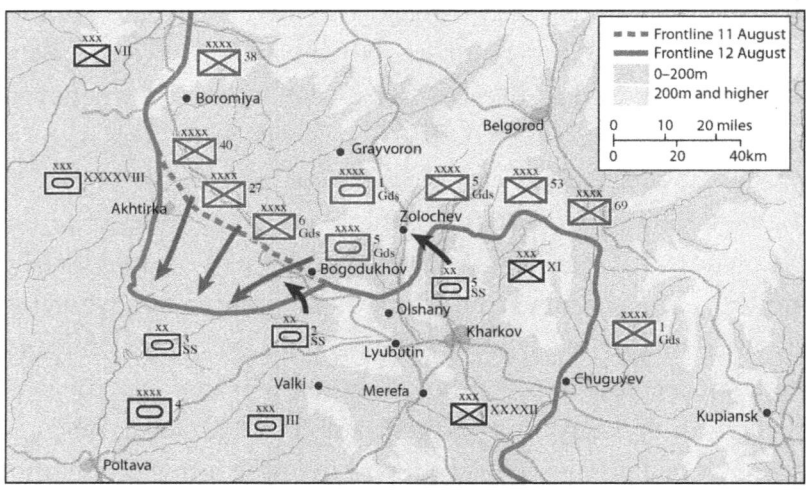

The Fourth Battle of Kharkov: 11–12 August 1943

Tank Corps. The *Totenkopf*'s assault guns were instrumental in blasting a way through the last line of Soviet resistance on 16 August. The trapped Russian troops formed themselves into small groups to try to infiltrate through the thinly held German lines during darkness. By this stage few German battalions mustered more than 200 frontline soldiers, so it was beyond their limited capabilities to draw tight nooses around bypassed pockets of Soviet troops. Some 4500 corpses, along with the remains of 21 T-34s and scores of artillery pieces and trucks, were found in the "pocket" as the Waffen-SS combed it for survivors.

Now the Waffen-SS divisions were ordered to turn northwards to chase away the remnants of the First Tank Army's shattered brigades. Both the *Totenkopf* and *Das Reich* Divisions used their last remaining Tigers to spearhead the drive. A strong Soviet rearguard action held up the advance for two days, with the Russians launching heavy tank counterattacks. The *Totenkopf* brought up its 88mm flak guns to destroy the T-34s that were now appearing in large numbers. *Wiking* Division's panzergrenadiers could not hold off the strong Russian infantry attacks, and so *Das Reich* had to send a panzergrenadier kampfgruppe to close a 1.6km (one-mile) breach in its sister division's front.

On 20 August, the *Totenkopf*'s panzer kampfgruppe forced a crossing of the river line and then turned westwards to start rolling up the Russian defences blocking the advance of the rest of III Panzer Corps. It lost several tanks in the operation, but eventually cleared out most of the main Soviet strong-points. Now the *Totenkopf* Division moved north to link up with the army's *Grossdeutschland* Panzergrenadier Division that was pushing westwards to cut off another Soviet incursion in the German line. This move trapped two Soviet rifle divisions and a tank corps in a mini pocket. Most of the trapped Soviet tanks were eventually destroyed, but almost all the infantry were able to escape into the forests.

In the swirling tank battles west of Kharkov, two Soviet tank armies had been all but destroyed, losing a total of more than 800 tanks in a two-week period. Soviet infantry divisions between Belgorod and Kharkov could now put only 4000 men into the frontline. III Panzer Corps' counterstroke had succeeded beyond the wildest dreams of its commanders. The price for the victor was heavy, though. German panzer divisions now averaged less than 30 operational tanks and assault guns each, while panzergrenadier battalions counted their frontline fighting strength in terms of dozens of men rather than hundreds.

With its attack to the west of Kharkov thwarted, the Soviet High Command now decided to switch the main effort of its offensive to the city itself. The Seventh Guards and Fifty-Seventh Armies were launched forward with support from the First Tank and Fifth Guards Tank Armies. They boasted a combined armoured force of more than 500 tanks, and had soon pushed the five weak infantry divisions of the German XI Corps back into a narrow horseshoe-shaped defensive line around the outskirts of the city. To protect the vulnerable flanks of the city, every available 88mm flak gun and assault gun was deployed to hold off the Soviet assault. Even with these deployments, though, the German commander in the city was not confident that he could hold out and he requested immediate reinforcements. After its successful operations to the west, *Das Reich* could be freed for the mission. SS Panzer Regiment 2 had also just been reinforced by its 1st Battalion, with 71 new Panther tanks, and they were soon on their way to bolster the defence of Kharkov.

Das Reich's panzer regiment and assault gun battalion were posted to the northwest sector of the city to guard the suspected approach route of the Fifth Guards Tank Army through a series of ripe corn and sunflower fields. Heavy air raids by Stuka diver-bombers and minefields broke up the tank formations of the Fifth Guards Tank Army's attack on 18 August. Marshal Pavel Rotmistrov called off his attacks, and was forced to reorganize his plan of assault for the next day. An infantry battalion infiltrated through the cornfields during the night and surprised a German artillery battery, which was only overrun after the crews had removed the breech-blocks of their guns and then retreated to safety. The Soviet infantry pressed on, and almost broke into XI Corps' command post before a German infantry kampfgruppe was able to trap the Russians in a small wood.

As dawn broke, small groups of Soviet tanks started to use ravines and stream beds to move through the cornfields to attack the German frontline. Waiting for them were the dug-in 88mm flak guns, along with 71 Panthers, 25 assault guns, 32 Panzer IVs and Tigers of the *Das Reich* Division. Wave after wave of T-34s tried to charge out of the cornfields to try to cross the few hundred metres to close with the main German defence line. During the course of the day the Germans claimed 184 T-34s destroyed by their guns.

Undeterred by these losses, Rotmistrov drove his men and tanks forward on 19 August. They tried to push down the railway line into the north of Kharkov. The result was the same, with the Panthers and 88mm flak guns destroying tanks at a range of 2000m (6561ft). Few Soviet tank crews even got within range to return fire before their T-34s were turned into raging infernos. On this day, the Germans claimed 154 Russian tanks destroyed.

During the following day, the Red armour laid low and prepared for another attack. Once darkness fell, hundreds of Russian tanks surged forward through the cornfields. The panzer gunners could only see their targets in the light of muzzle flashes from other tanks or antitank guns. The Russians kept coming forward. Soon they were among the German tanks, and the two armoured forces started firing at each other at point-blank range. Some tank crews even rammed each other in the chaos. After dawn the German line was secure, with 80 more Russian tanks burning in front of *Das Reich*'s position. XI Corps, however, had to order tank and infantry sweeps to clear out pockets of Soviet troops that had infiltrated behind their lines. Flamethrower teams and 88mm flak guns were used to hunt down and kill the dozen or so Soviet tanks that were still loose behind German lines south of Kharkov.

The Soviet Fifty-Seventh Army was also pressing Kharkov from the southeast, and after it had cut the railway line into the city it was only a matter of time before it fell. By 21 August, the Kharkov garrison had all but exhausted its reserves of artillery ammunition. Manstein now gave the order to pull out of the city. During for the next 48 hours, the Germans withdrew their troops and started blowing up supply dumps to stop them falling into the hands of the Red Army. During the early hours of 23 August, Soviet troops drove out the last German rearguards and raised the Red Banner over Dzerzhinsky Square.

The vicious fighting around Kharkov had exhausted both the Soviet and German armies. For three weeks the northern wing of Army Group South had been able to stabilize its front. In the south, the weak Sixth Army now became the focus of Soviet attention. It lasted only a few weeks under relentless pressure

THE FÜHRER'S FIRE BRIGADE

before its units were streaming westwards in disorder. This defeat exposed the northern wing of Manstein's army group. With no reserves available to plug the gap, Hitler reluctantly agreed on 15 September to allow Manstein to pull his troops back behind the Dnieper.

The *Wiking*, *Das Reich* and *Totenkopf* Divisions were now operating under the command of the Eighth Army (formerly Army Detachment *Kempf*) during the withdrawal back to the Dnieper at Kremenchung. The three once-proud Waffen-SS panzer divisions were now badly weakened by almost three months of constant combat. They barely mustered 25 tanks and a dozen assault guns each, while their panzergrenadier battalions often had no more than 100 men each. Starting on 22 September the withdrawal began, with the Eighth Army's divisions falling back from one defence line to another, according to a very deliberate plan. The *Totenkopf* and *Das Reich* Divisions formed the first rearguard, before falling back behind army divisions. This leap-frogging continued until the *Totenkopf* and three army divisions held an inner defensive line around the city of Kremenchung on 28 August. The final rear-guard held out for two more days and allowed most of the Eighth Army's transport to escape across the mighty Dnieper.

In mid-October 1943, the Soviets renewed their offensive in the southern Ukraine. After crossing the River Dnieper, the Red Army rolled over the weak LVII Corps with another huge tank armada and headed westward towards Krivoi Rog. Field Marshal Manstein again gathered his panzer fire brigade to stabilize the front. XXXX Panzer Corps, with the *Totenkopf* Division as its spearhead, scythed into the flank of the Soviet assault force. Six weak German panzer divisions smashed two Soviet tank corps and nine rifle divisions, taking 5300 prisoners and destroying 300 tanks in the process. The *Totenkopf* Division remained on station in the Dnieper bend for the remainder of 1943, launching one counterattack after another to maintain the German line. It had a major success at the end of November when its antitank guns and panzers blocked a Soviet tank force, destroying 245 T-34s in a three-day period. Another big Soviet attack then seized Krivoi Rog and the *Totenkopf* was thrown into action again to retake the town. Two more counterattacks during December blunted further Soviet attacks.

These battles cost the *Totenkopf* dearly, though, and by this time it was approaching breaking point. The *Das Reich* and *Wiking* Divisions were in a similar position. After retreating over the Dnieper, the *Wiking* Division was reinforced with additional volunteers from occupied Scandinavian countries and Belgium. *Das Reich* was to be pulled out of Russia and rebuilt in France. SS-Obersturmbannführer Heinz Lammerding, however, remained behind with a kampfgruppe to help hold the Dnieper line to the south of Kiev. In only a few weeks it would find itself fighting for its life.

Chapter 7
DEATH ON THE DNIEPER

Waffen-SS panzers and the battles to hold the Ukraine.

Soviet war production was running in high gear by the third year of the war on the Eastern Front, turning out more than 20,000 tanks and heavy assault guns during 1943 alone. This was twice the rate Germans industry could produce, and by this stage in the war Adolf Hitler had to contend not only with the Red Army but also Anglo-American forces in Italy and a huge US-led invasion army poised to land in northern France. In the final months of 1943, the Eastern Front was at the bottom of the Führer's priorities as he tried to build up the much-vaunted Atlantic Wall to hold back the expected cross-Channel invasion from Great Britain. In the East, the so-called "Eastern Rampart" along the mighty River Dnieper was not much more than a propaganda myth.

This was cruelly exposed in early November 1943 when the Soviet High Command launched a massive offensive to seize Kiev, the Ukrainian capital. The Red Army pushed across the Dnieper and threatened to open a breach between the Wehrmacht's Army Group South and its neighbour to the north, Army Group Centre. The brunt of the attack fell on the 11 infantry divisions of the German Fourth Panzer Army. These divisions had been fighting without relief or reinforcements since the summer, and most could barely deploy a regiment's worth of troops into the frontline. When 20 Russian infantry divisions, backed by four tank and one cavalry corps, rolled forward, the German VII Corps was lucky to get out of Kiev without being surrounded and wiped out. Two weak army panzer divisions failed to even dent the Soviet armoured juggernaut as it rolled westwards for 112km (70 miles), capturing the key railway junctions of Fastov and Zhitomir. More than 1000 Soviet tanks were loose behind German lines, and they threatened to turn south and roll up all of Field Marshal Erich von Manstein's army group. Disaster looked certain if action was not taken fast.

Hitler had already released the 1st SS Panzer Division *Leibstandarte Adolf Hitler*, as the premier Waffen-SS armoured formation was now titled, from its occupation duties in Italy for service on the Eastern Front, when the Soviet offensive burst around Kiev. The new crisis created a sense of urgency for the officers of the division, which had now been rested and refitted during its three-month break away from the bloodbath in the East.

The *Leibstandarte*, with its powerful panzer regiment equipped with 95 Panther, 96 Panzer IV and 27 Tiger I tanks, would provide the heavy armoured punch for the counteroffensive being planned by Manstein. Two army panzer divisions, the veteran 1st Panzer and the newly formed 25th Panzer, would support the attack. The 1st Panzer boasted 95 Panzer IVs and 76 Panthers, while the 25th Panzer had 93 Panzer IVs and an attached heavy tank battalion armed with 25 Tiger Is. Going into action alongside this force were elements of three other weak panzer divisions: the Waffen-SS *Das Reich* Division with 22 Panzer IVs, six Panzer IIIs and 10 Tigers, and two Army divisions – the 7th and 19th Panzer – which mustered only 40 tanks between them.

Difficult tank terrain

To lead the counterattack, Manstein appointed the veteran army panzer commander General Hermann Balck. His XXXXVIII Panzer Corps in theory would have almost 500 tanks available for the operation, but they would take several weeks to assemble and be ready for action.

The terrain west of Kiev was very different from the open steppes to the east, with huge forests stretching for kilometres across the countryside. Small Ukrainian towns sat on most of the road junctions and around a number of strategic bridges. A number of key railway lines ran through the region, and it was vital for both sides to control them in order to transport troops and supplies. The poor state of the road network further increased the importance of the railways. Throughout November 1943, temperatures were hovering just above freezing, which meant sudden thaws and rain turned most roads and fields into thick mud quagmires that sucked in even tracked vehicles. The arrival of freezing winter weather was keenly anticipated by all Eastern Front tank commanders, because it would enable rapid movement off roads across the frozen ground – a panzer general's dream.

At the end of the first week of November, Manstein ordered his counterattack force to assemble around the town of Fastov, which at that time was located on the left flank of the Soviet incursion into the German lines. It would still be another week before the panzer strike force was ready, however, and in the meantime it was imperative that its assembly area was secure. The only forces available, the advance elements of the 25th Panzer Division and the *Das Reich* Division, were hastily thrown into action. They suffered heavy losses when their armour was delayed and the lorry borne panzergrenadiers found themselves locked in battle with hundreds of T-34s. Their holding action bought Balck time to gather his divisions, though, and they were sent rolling forward on 15 November. The Russians had not been in position long enough to dig-in their pak-fronts, so to the *Leibstandarte*'s panzer crews the advance resembled the "good old days" around Kharkov the previous spring. SS-Sturmbannführer Joachim Peiper was now leading the division's panzer regiment. He was soon to be in the centre of the action.

The *Leibstandarte* Division was to be one of two strike groups, which were going to cut into the flank of the Soviet First Ukrainian Front to surround and destroy the Third Tank Army's armoured groups. The *Das Reich* and 25th Panzer Divisions were to screen the *Leibstandarte*'s left flank as it moved northwards.

Two powerful kampfgruppen were formed for the Waffen-SS advance, built around each of the *Leibstandarte*'s panzergrenadier regiments. Each one had a panzer battalion and assault

DEATH ON THE DNIEPER

guns attached to spearhead their advance. With Tigers and Sturmgeschütz (StuG) IIIs leading the way, the kampfgruppen easily punched holes in the thinly held Soviet front and headed north. The 2nd SS Panzergrenadier Regiment soon ran into heavy resistance from two Soviet tank corps and a cavalry corps in the large town of Brusilov. To bypass this road-block the division's Panther battalion led the 1st SS Panzergrenadier Regiment on a detour to the west. They rolled over a Soviet rifle division's headquarters and then swung east again to strike at Brusilov from the north. This kampfgruppe formed the inner ring of the pincer, while the army's 1st Panzer Division advanced in parallel and then swung south to form the outer ring of steel around the Russian tank force. German assault columns dodged off the road network to weave through forests to find the best

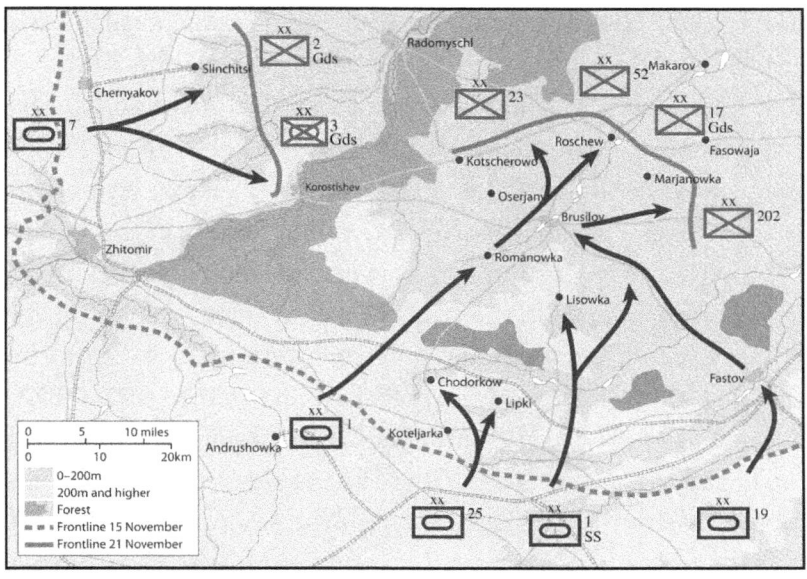

The Attack on Radomyschl: 15–21 August 1943

149

way to surround the isolated groups of Soviet tanks and antitank guns which were thrown in their way.

Heavy Soviet counterattacks were thrown at the *Leibstandarte*'s pincers, but the Waffen-SS men pressed on. Speed was their best ally. As the German panzer units closed in on Brusilov, the Soviet defence became more desperate. Several Soviet brigades were thrown into action to stop the *Leibstandarte*'s wide pincer move. Tigers, Panthers and StuG IIIs saw off these attacks, knocking out scores of T-34s in the process.

A final push was made on 22 November to close the ring, with Tiger tanks leading the advance of the southern pincer. They blasted their way through a pak-front holding open the Russians' escape route, knocking out 24 tanks and two assault guns. Peiper, with a kampfgruppe of Panzer IVs and panzergrenadiers riding in armoured halftracks, led the advance northwards during the following afternoon, to link up with the advance guard of the army's 1st Panzer Division which was probing the northern suburbs of Brusilov. The impetuous Peiper raced forward, but he was held up by huge swamps north of the town. His kampfgruppe then destroyed nine T-34s and 24 antitank guns during this sweep, and saw off another Russian attempt to break through to the forces now trapped in Brusilov, destroying six more tanks in the process. Trapped in the pocket were elements of seven major Soviet units. German Army divisions were used to comb the pocket – they cleared out several thousand prisoners and 3000 Russian dead littered the battlefield. The Germans claimed 153 tanks and more than 320 artillery pieces destroyed. Thousands more Russian troops escaped through the swamps to freedom.

The *Leibstandarte* Division was now re-grouped for a further push northwards, to the heavily defended town of Radomyschl.

DEATH ON THE DNIEPER

Heavy frost meant the division was able to concentrate its dispersed forces for their operation that started on 29 November. Peiper's panzer regiment and the reconnaissance battalion led the way. His Tigers punched a hole through a thick pak-front south of Radomyschl, but as resistance stiffened the attack was called off. A new plan was being devised to prise open the Red Army's new south-facing front.

XXXXVIII Panzer Corps was to move 64km (40 miles) westwards in front of the Russians, and then hit their exposed western flank, rolling up their new frontline of antitank guns and dug-in tanks. German infantry divisions were to stage diversionary attacks along the whole of the Soviet line to keep the enemy's attention focused on the south. With the Ukraine now firmly in the grip of a heavy winter frost, the *Leibstandarte* Division moved at night, undetected by Soviet reconnaissance patrols, to its jump-off point north of Zhitomir on 6 December. Peiper was again to lead the attack with his panzer regiment, armoured troop carrier battalion and the reconnaissance battalion. For six hours Peiper advanced unopposed into the enemy's rear area, rolling up artillery batteries and supply dumps. His Tigers ambushed several large truck convoys during the advance and shot them up.

The Waffen-SS tanks pressed home their advantage during the following day, but then ran out of fuel during the afternoon and had to be re-supplied before the advance could continue. Stung by criticism of his logistical problems the previous day, Peiper pushed his men forward with a vengeance on 7 December, covering more than 32km (20 miles) and cutting the road north out of Radomyschl. He then pushed southwards to reach the outskirts of the town, before turning east to close the ring around what was left of the Soviet Sixtieth Army. The division's panzergrenadiers now caught up with the panzer spearhead to form an iron ring around the town, and turn back furious attempts by the Soviets to force a relief column through to their trapped men.

For almost a week, the *Leibstandarte* Division held the ring around the Russian forces trapped in Radomyschl. The division's panzers were also used to force back Russian troops to the north of the town, and smash the remaining enemy armoured reserves in the area. The advance was successful at first, but Peiper's tank crews got bogged down in a series of costly but inconclusive engagements.

Almost a month of intense combat had taken its toll on the mighty *Leibstandarte* Division. Its tank strength now stood at some 20 tanks fit for action, with almost 200 tanks under repair. The panzergrenadier regiments were equally stretched, and each could only muster 500 men fit to fight.

Another Soviet tank force was now located gathering to the northwest around Meleni, and so Balck called off his attacks on Radomyschl. The *Leibstandarte* and 1st Panzer Divisions were ordered to launch another of the general's favourite pincer moves. In two night-time road marches they were moved north to assembly areas to the west of the Soviet force, to be ready for action on 19 December. From the east the 7th Panzer Division attacked to close the noose. *Leibstandarte* repair crews had struggled to get seven Tigers, 12 Panthers, 33 Panzer IVs and 18 StuG IIIs ready for the assault. The attack rolled forward under a barrage from 30 artillery batteries and scores of Nebelwerfer launchers. At first the *Leibstandarte* panzergrenadiers surprised the Russians and cleared out a score of trenches with little opposition. Then the panzer kampfgruppe moved forward until it ran into a huge pak-front of antitank guns. The attack got bogged down, and so the Waffen-SS division brought up its heavy 88mm Flak guns to try to win the deadly duel. XXXXVIII Panzer Corps' senior staff were now starting to realize that they might had taken on more than their three weakened divisions could handle. Three Soviet armoured corps and elements of four infantry corps were in the salient being pushed in by the three German divisions.

During the following morning, the *Leibstandarte*'s panzer kampfgruppe pushed forward again with its Tigers in the lead, and it made some excellent gains until it started to encounter heavy Soviet tank attacks. Waffen-SS losses mounted, until the division had only 20 tanks left fit for action, including three

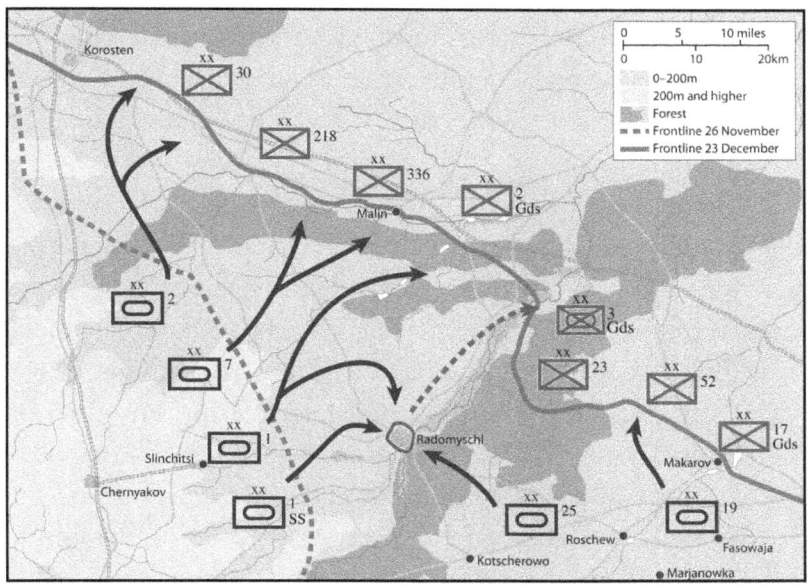

The Attack on Radomyschl: 26 November–23 December 1943

Tigers, by the end of the day. It accounted for 17 T-34s, four assault guns and 44 artillery pieces destroyed. The following morning one panzer company of six tanks fended off a huge Soviet tank attack, destroying 21 T-34s in the desperate battle. By the afternoon the *Leibstandarte*'s panzer regiment pulled its last remaining operational tanks out of the battle.

XXXXVIII Panzer Corps could only maintain its attack for two days, but it had inflicted big losses on the Soviets, with the 1st Panzer Division smashing a two corps-sized attack and knocking out 68 tanks on 22 December. The following day Balck halted the attack so he could use his three panzer divisions to form a mobile reserve, ready to parry another Soviet attack force that was gathering to the south in XXIV Panzer Corps' sector. During the previous two months Balck and his elite panzer divisions claimed to have destroyed or captured 700 Soviet tanks and 668 antitank guns. The size of the Soviet armada being gathered west of Kiev – more than 1000 tanks – would prove just too big for Balck's men to hold, though.

The storm broke on 24 December 1943. The Soviet juggernaut brushed aside the *Das Reich* Division and the army's 8th and 19th Panzer Divisions, before heading southwest towards Manstein's headquarters at Vinnitsa, 80km (50 miles) away. Balck and his staff spent a frantic day trying to disengage XXXXVIII Panzer Corps from the Meleni Front. His chief of staff, Major-General F.W. Mellenthin, personally had to lead a scratch kampfgruppe of 25 tanks from the *Leibstandarte* and 1st Panzer Divisions to destroy a dangerous break-in on the corps' right flank and allow it to break free for new operations.

While the 1st Panzer Division struck out to the east of

DEATH ON THE DNIEPER

Zhitomir to re-establish contact with the cut-off panzer divisions of XXIV Panzer Corps, the *Leibstandarte* Division was ordered to head south through the city to block the Soviet advance.

Holding Zhitomir
An improvised defence force of army assault guns and artillery units was mustered to hold the towns of Berdichev and Kazatin, directly in the path of the Soviet advance. A deep antitank ditch had been dug outside the towns, and this formed the core of the defence line.

Heavy traffic jams of retreating logistic units prevented the *Leibstandarte* and 7th Panzer Divisions getting through to Zhitomir until 26 December, from where they were ordered to push south to retake Kazatin. The advance at last began on the following morning. Balck was with the forward tanks, and was amazed to see 800 T-34s driving across the plain in front of him. He immediately ordered his tanks to attack, but the small force just bounced off the mass of Russian armour in spite of disabling 78 Soviet tanks. The Russian force rolled on into Kazatin later in the day. The 1st Panzer Division pushed south to retake the town and the *Leibstandarte* manoeuvred in front of Berdichev to stop a massive column of tanks heading towards it.

A frantic defence
A Waffen-SS Panther company with 13 tanks was deployed as the division's forward line. A dawn attack by a Soviet tank brigade was thwarted when the Panthers hit them in the flank and destroyed 19 T-34s, before scattering a Russian infantry column.

On 29 December the Russians attacked in strength, launching

more than 150 tanks along the length of the *Leibstandarte*'s front. That morning it could only get four Tigers, eight Panzer IVs, 17 Panthers, 15 StuG IIIs and four Marder self-propelled antitank guns into the line to meet the Soviet onslaught. Two assault guns and a couple of 88mm guns had to meet an attack by 40 T-34s. They knocked out nine of them, and then the intervention of a Tiger destroyed eight more, driving off the attack. A pair of Panthers saw off a breakthrough during the afternoon, and the 88mm flak guns also accounted for many T-34s. In total some 59 Russians tanks were knocked out in front of the division's line. During the early evening, however, a force of 65 enemy tanks had skirted round the northern end of the *Leibstandarte*'s line.

A Waffen-SS tank counterattack was ordered for the following morning to re-establish contact with the 7th Panzer Division in Zhitomir. The Waffen-SS held the line with grim determination during 30 December, but the pressure became unbearable on the final day of 1943. Hundreds of T-34s surged forward, to be met by a hail of fire which knocked out 25 of them. As darkness fell, the division was ordered to fall back as part of a deliberate withdrawal by XXXXVIII Panzer Corps from Berdichev. During the five days of the battle the Russians had lost more than 200 tanks in front of Balck's corps front. But the Germans had also lost equipment, which could not easily be replaced.

The *Leibstandarte* Division was pulled out of the line near Berdichev in the first days of January 1944, and then moved north to try to close a gap in the front between XXXXVIII Panzer Corps and LIX Corps. For a two-week period the division fought a series of tank duels to neutralize small incursions behind German lines. Its panzer kampfgruppe made daily forays, with the small panzer detachment of the *Das Reich* kampfgruppe, stalking any T-34s that were roaming the winter battlefield. SS-Untersturmführer Michael Wittmann earned himself a personal radio message of congratulation from Balck himself for destroying 37 T-34s and seven assault guns in a single engagement that drove off a Soviet incursion into a neighbouring army infantry division.

By the time the *Leibstandarte* Division was pulled out of the line for rest and refitting itself, it had claimed 288 Soviet tanks destroyed since the start of its Christmas offensive. Among the Soviet prisoners taken had been a number young boys and old men. Many in Army Group South believed that this was proof that the Soviets were beginning to exhaust their vast reserves of manpower. This optimism was short-lived, though.

Away from the frontline, the *Leibstandarte* Division was soon able to repair its damaged vehicles, and on 21 January 1944 it had 22 Panthers, 25 Panzer IVs, one Tiger and 27 StuG IIIs ready for action. All these vehicles would soon be needed on the Eastern Front.

Chapter 8
KESSEL BATTLES

The Cherkassy and Kamenets Podolsk Pockets.

Kessel is the German word for 'kettle'. It is also the German military term for a 'battle of encirclement'. The analogy is appropriate. Once caught in a pocket by enemy pincers, any trapped troops are put under increasing pressure until a boiling point is reached. In the face of dwindling supplies, the trapped troops would either have to break out or face destruction.

Weakened by a steady stream of losses since the Battle of Kursk in July 1943, the Wehrmacht's Eastern Front was in tatters by January 1944. It was held by a rag-tag collection of divisions that were lucky to each be able to put 5000 fit soldiers into their frontline trenches. As for mobile reserves, they were also all but exhausted. Even the elite panzer divisions of the Waffen-SS were lucky if they could scrape together 30 battered and worn-out tanks that could be defined as 'combat ready'. It was only a matter of time before the Soviet High Command exploited this weakness, and started to chop up the German Army Group South into small chunks and annihilate it. Field Marshal Erich von Manstein had a reputation for being Germany's master strategist, but by January 1944 even he was running out of tricks to "magic" his battered frontline back together again.

The Soviet breakthrough southwest of Kiev during December 1943 pushed the German Fourth Panzer Army back over 160km (100 miles), leaving the Eighth Army's right flank dangerously exposed. In January 1944, it was the only German formation with a foothold on the southern banks of the River Dnieper. True to form, Hitler refused to let it withdraw to safety, and it was therefore only a matter of time before the Soviet High Command closed the net around it. The core of the Eighth Army's defence was the Waffen-SS *Wiking* Panzergrenadier Division. Usually, it had only a dozen Panzer IIIs, eight Panzer IVs and four Sturmgeschütz (StuG) IIIs ready for action on any day during January 1944. The division also boasted the Walloon Assault Brigade made up of Nazi Flemish volunteers from northern Belgium.

The Soviets made their first attempt to surround the Eighth Army in early January, with another steamroller offensive aimed at smashing XLVII Panzer Corps deployed to defend Kirovograd, which protected the route to the German rear. More than 600 Russian tanks opened a huge breach in the German line and trapped four German divisions in the sprawling industrial city. "Kirovograd sounds too much like Stalingrad for my liking", was the comment of the garrison commander, who took advantage of a breakdown in radio communications with higher command to order his troops to march to freedom. They successfully broke out with all their tanks and heavy artillery. The line was rebuilt after Manstein moved in two fresh divisions to mount a counterattack. Leading this effort was the Waffen-SS *Totenkopf* Division, which had been brought up from the lower Dnieper. Just as the Soviets were preparing for a final push, the *Totenkopf* burst upon them and scattered several Russian divisions. This was only a temporary respite, though.

Manstein now tried to turn the tables on the Soviet First Tank Army that was pushing southwards into the Eighth Army's exposed left flank. He pulled together a scratch force of three 'divisions', under army panzer General Hermann Breith, and launched them eastwards into the flank of the Russian tank force. Heavy mud delayed the deployment of the *Leibstandarte* Division into position to lead Breith's III Panzer Corps. Backed by fire from the Wehrmacht's only artillery division, the Waffen-SS troops sliced into the flank of the Soviet spearhead. Heavy mud seriously impeded the progress of men and machines, but with its Tigers in the lead the division swept all before it. By 28 January it had closed the ring around several Russian divisions. The Germans claimed 8000 Russians dead, 701 tanks destroyed and 5436 prisoners.

This success was occurring at the same time as another Soviet advance was moving to trap the German Eighth Army on 24 January. Two armoured pincers sliced into the thinly held flanks of the army and met up on 28 January to close the noose around 56,000 men of the German XI and XLII Corps, forming what has since become known as the Korsun, or Cherkassy, Pocket. The only German armoured unit in the pocket was the *Wiking* Division.

KESSEL BATTLES

Just as at Stalingrad, Hitler ordered the troops in the pocket to stand firm and wait for a rescue force to restore the front behind them. In the meantime, an air bridge would keep them supplied with food, fuel and ammunition. It was a fantasy. Soviet fighters started to take a huge toll on the Luftwaffe supply aircraft. On the ground, more than 500 Soviet tanks were ringing the pocket, and Manstein could only muster four worn-out panzer divisions to mount a rescue mission. Hitler would give him no fresh troops from Western Europe because of the Anglo-American threat to France. Breith, meanwhile, was ordered to complete his operation against the encircled Russian force to the west and then batter his way through to the Eighth Army.

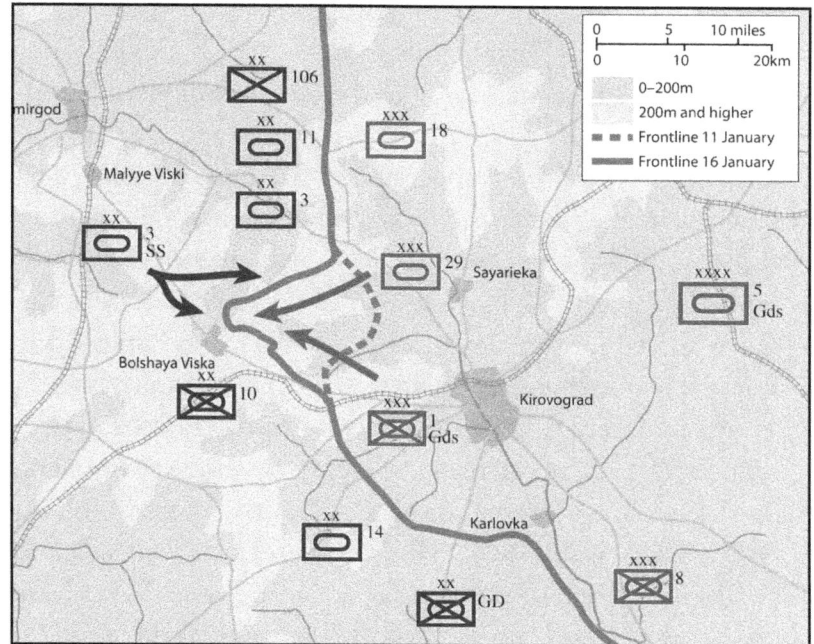

The Breakthrough at Kirovograd: 11–16 January 1944

WAFFEN-SS PANZERS: EASTERN FRONT

The army's 16th and 17th Panzer Divisions spearheaded the break-in operation, with the composite "Bake" Heavy Panzer Regiment in the lead. This unit was at this time the most powerful German tank unit on the Eastern Front, boasting 47 Panther and 34 Tiger I tanks, supported by armoured infantry and self-propelled units. Attacking northwards on 4 February in an attempt to turn the tables on the Soviet tank force and trap it in a pocket, the rescue force at first made good progress across frozen ground. A sudden thaw now turned the battlefield into a quagmire. III Panzer Corps' advance literally got bogged down. Wheeled fuel tankers and ammunition trucks just could not move. Even tracked vehicles had difficulties. At times fuel for the tanks even had to be carried forward to the front in buckets or cans. The *Leibstandarte* Division battled on for 32km (20 miles). Its Tiger company destroyed 26 Soviet tanks as it established a bridgehead over the River Gniloy Tikich on 8 February 1944.

With its northward advance stalled, III Panzer Corps now moved the *Leibstandarte* Division and the army's 1st Panzer Division southwards so they could attack directly eastwards towards the pocket. This switch confused the Soviets, and the advance moved forward again, with the Waffen-SS on the left and the 1st Panzer on right. Again frost helped the tank advance, and the 1st Panzer Division was able to throw a bridgehead over the Gniloy Tikich at Lyssinka, only 8km (five miles) from the trapped troops. A huge pak-front of 52 antitank guns and 80 T-34s barred its way, though. The 16th Panzer Division and the Bake Regiment tried to outflank the enemy defences by pushing north, but they were soon stopped by heavy enemy fire.

As the *Leibstandarte* Division tried to keep up with the

advance, it was hit by huge Soviet tank attacks. First V Rifle Corps, followed by XVI Tank Corps, surged forward. It was all the understrength Waffen-SS division could do to hold off the non-stop attacks that swept forward out of the thick forests. The division's Tiger company was at the centre of the defence, knocking out scores of Russian tanks as they streamed forward.

The battle went on for days. Soviet tanks washed around the small German units holding open the 1.6km- (one-mile-) wide corridor eastwards. Several times the Russians cut the corridor, and counter-attacks had to be mounted to clear out their infantry and tanks. By 16 February, the 1st Panzer Division, helped by *Leibstandarte* panzergrenadiers, was holding on to its bridgehead by its fingernails. Only 60 men and a dozen Panther tanks were across the river, holding off daily attacks by V Guards Tanks Corps. III Panzer Corps just did not have enough strength to mount the final push to open a corridor to the trapped troops. During the afternoon, Manstein ordered XI and XLII Corps to break out west that evening. He avoided consulting the Führer's headquarters to prevent his orders being countermanded.

Inside the pocket, artillery General Wilhelm Stemmermann was not going to repeat the mistakes of Field Marshal Freidrich Paulus at Stalingrad, and he immediately prepared to follow Manstein's orders. There was no time to lose.

The trapped troops were organized into three assault columns and a rearguard for the break-out. *Wiking* formed the southern column. Its last remaining Panzer IIIs and StuG IIIs led the advance, which began at 23:00 hours on 16 February. The first assault went in silently, with German infantry eliminating Soviet sentries by bayoneting them. This established paths through the Soviet inner ring, and then the *Wiking's* tanks fanned out to provide flank protection for the ragged column.

The other two columns, made up of two infantry divisions, used guile to slip through the Russian lines to link up with 1st Panzer Division. *Wiking's* column soon ran into trouble when a storm of Russian machine-gun and tank fire started to rake it. SS-Obergruppenführer Herbert Gille, *Wiking's* commander, ordered one of his battalions to deal with this threat, while the rest of his division skirted around to the south of the Russian blocking position. When the Waffen-SS grenadiers reached the Gniloy Tikich, they abandoned all their heavy equipment and swam the freezing river before finding safety.

It was then the rearguard's turn to move out, and soon the two infantry divisions were being bombarded from the blocking position that had hampered *Wiking's* escape attempt. They too broke and ran for the Gniloy Tikich. The few kilometres to the river were soon littered with abandoned trucks, cars, wagons, artillery pieces and tanks, as well as the bodies of 15,000 dead Germans. Among them was their commander, Stemmermann, who died when a tank shell ripped into the wagon he was travelling in.

Throughout the night and into the morning, the pathetic survivors of the pocket staggered past the men of the 1st Panzer and *Leibstandarte* Divisions. The hardened panzer troops were shocked at the poor morale of the survivors. They started to talk about 'Kessel shock' – a penetrating fear of capture by the Soviets that overrode normal discipline and led to the breakdown of unit cohesion in time of crisis.

KESSEL BATTLES

The 1st Panzer Division held its bridgehead open for two more days, though only some 30,000 men found their way to German lines. The *Wiking* Division was shattered, and was now reduced to less than half of its established strength. Only 600 troops out of the Walloon Brigade's 2000 men escaped.

The survivors were soon shipped away from the front, and III Panzer Corps pulled back to establish a defence line ready to repel the inevitable next Soviet offensive. During late February Manstein reorganized his remaining panzer divisions as best he could, but there was now a feeling that the next Soviet onslaught would be unstoppable, wherever it struck.

Stalin now sent his strategic genius, Marshal Georgi Zhukov, to supervise the final destruction of Manstein's army group. He was to personally lead a pincer attack into the left wing of Manstein's front, and another attack on the other flank would eventually seal the trap around the First and Fourth Panzer Armies. If the attack succeeded, 200,000 Germans would be cut off and destroyed in the biggest Kessel battle since Stalingrad.

As usual, the Russians massed huge breakthrough forces close to their chosen pressure points. Whole divisions of artillery blasted the German lines for days, and then several hundred T-34s were launched forward to drive over the ruins. The targets were two weak infantry corps, which soon folded when the Soviet attacks went in on 4 and 5 March 1944. In a matter of days Zhukov's tank corps covered more than 160km (100 miles), and most of Manstein's army group – 22 divisions – found itself cut off in a huge Kessel or pocket centred around the town of Kamenets Podolsk. The cut-off troops included the cream of the Wehrmacht's panzer divisions, as well as both the *Leibstandarte* and *Das Reich* Waffen-SS Divisions. Command of the trapped

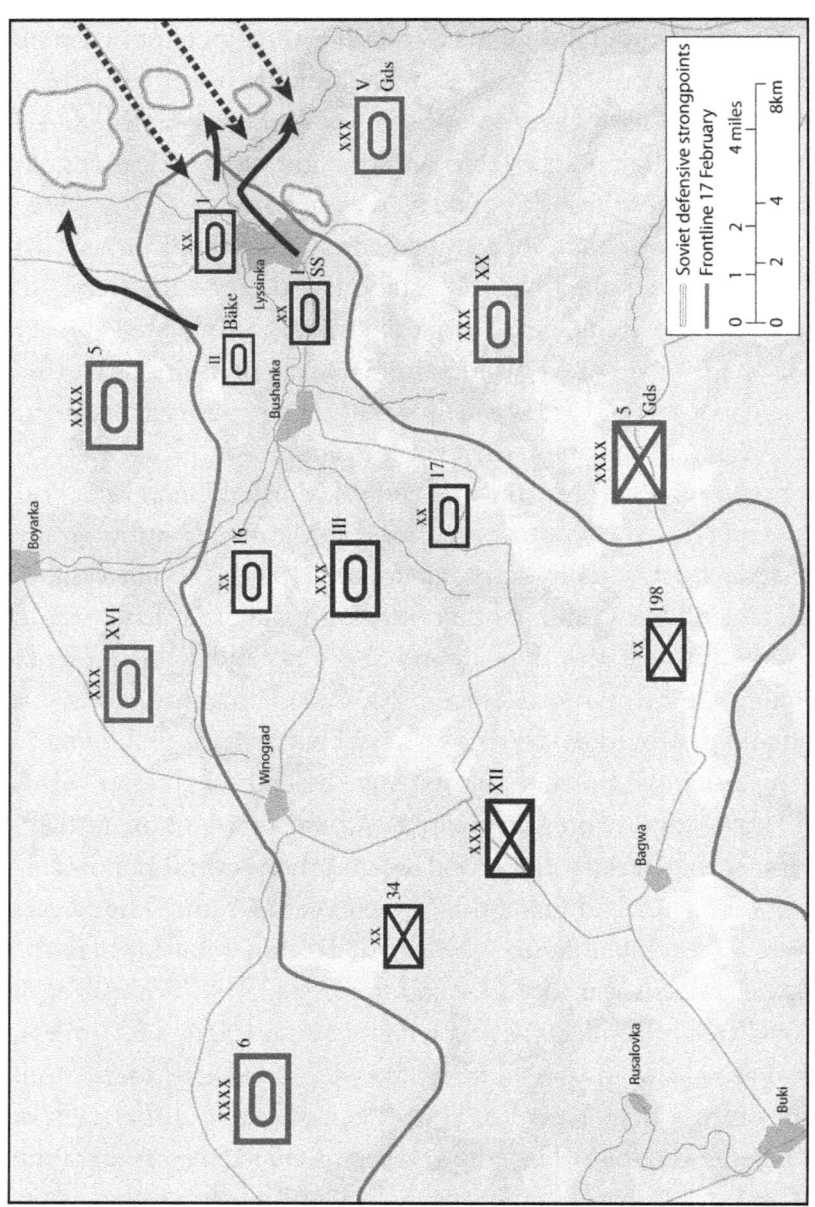

The Cherkassy Pocket: Relief attempts, 16–20 February 1944

KESSEL BATTLES

troops fell to the First Panzer Army's commander, Colonel-General Hans Hube. The one-armed tank commander had actually served under Paulus at Stalingrad, and he would soon put into practice some of the lessons he had learned in that Kessel battle. Just before Stalingrad fell, Hitler ordered Hube to be evacuated because he had earmarked him for rapid promotion.

Still serving with III Panzer Corps, the *Leibstandarte* Division was in the path of Zhukov's massive southward pincer. With only a dozen operational Panthers and a handful of other tanks and assault guns to hand, the division had no hope of stopping the several hundred Russian tanks that streamed through the breach in the Eastern Front. The Waffen-SS played an instrumental part in rescuing several army infantry divisions that looked as if they might be overrun. At this point it became the cornerstone of the west-facing front of the pocket. Over on the eastern edge of the pocket, the *Das Reich* kampfgruppe was in an equally precarious position, with six Panthers, five Panzer IVs and four StuG IIIs ready for action. The small *Das Reich* contingent desperately fought alongside a number of improvised kampfgruppen to hold a firm front facing eastwards, as more than 400 Russian tanks battered at Hube's beleaguered command.

Strategic withdrawal

Hube and Manstein, however, were determined not to repeat the mistakes made at Stalingrad, which had signed the death warrant of the Sixth Army. They first of all refused to follow Hitler's orders and declare the pocket a 'fortress', one that had to be defended to the last man. Hube's pocket was going to be a "mobile pocket" – it would keep moving so the Russians would not be able to trap it, and then concentrate their forces against it.

For more than two weeks Hube kept his army moving southwards, and then westwards to keep the Russians guessing about the exact location of his divisions. Air supply was organized properly, with each division having its own Luftwaffe team who set up improvised airstrips each day. Fuel and ammunition were flown in and the wounded evacuated. By this stage of the war the Luftwaffe had finally mastered this type of operation, and the air bridge provided Hube's men with just enough supplies for them to keep fighting and moving. The continual movement was also good for morale, and Hube's army did not suffer any of the panics that were seen in the Cherkassy Pocket.

The obvious escape route for Hube's men was to head south, where a number of bridges over the River Dniester into Romania remained open. Zhukov therefore concentrated the bulk of his tanks against these crossings, rather than reinforcing the eastward-facing defences of his pincers. Manstein devised a plan for Hube to attack directly westwards, cutting through the Russian lines to escape and meet up with rescue forces moving east.

Hitler hated the plan because it gave up huge amounts of territory. For days he sat on his hands and refused to make a decision. On 24 March Manstein threatened to issue the breakout orders anyway, unless Hitler agreed to his plan. On this rare occasion the Führer backed down. Field Marshal Manstein got his freedom of movement and his reinforcements – II SS Panzer Corps. It would begin to move to the Eastern Front from France immediately, with the two well-equipped but unblooded Waffen-SS Divisions: the 9th Hohenstaufen and the 10th Frundsberg Panzer Divisions.

KESSEL BATTLES

Inside the pocket, two assault groups were formed to batter past the Soviet defences. The *Leibstandarte*, then part of Kampfgruppe Mauss, fell back from its positions on the western flank of the pocket and deployed as part of the flank guard. As part of Corps Group von Chevallerei, the elite Waffen-SS division helped hold open the escape corridor for almost 12 days against repeated attacks by the Soviet Third Guards Tank Army. The *Das Reich* Division stayed as the rearguard on the eastern edge of the pocket.

Manstein's deception plan worked. Zhukov did not realize what was happening until it was too late, and he was only able to move one tank corps northwards in an attempt to stop the breakout. By 4 April 1944, the army's 1st and 6th Panzer Divisions were poised to attack the last line of Soviet troops blocking their escape route.

Central to Manstein's breakout plan was the deployment of II SS Panzer Corps to punch a corridor through from the west and take the pressure off Hube's hard-pressed troops in the pocket. On paper, II SS Panzer Corps was a formidable force, but its leaders and soldiers were largely untried in combat. Their commander, SS-Obergruppenführer Willi Bittrich, was one of the most professional officers in the Waffen-SS and he is most famous for the destruction of the British 1st Airborne Division at Arnhem in September 1944. Many of his divisional and regimental commanders were very raw, even though the individual soldiers of the corps showed plenty of Waffen-SS fighting spirit. Bittrich's corps boasted an impressive array of weaponry, with Hohenstaufen fielding 21 Panthers, 38 Panzer IVs, 44 StuG IIIs and 12 Marder self-propelled antitank guns, while Frundsberg could put 44 Panzer IVs and 49 StuG IIIs into action.

By 3 April, Bittrich's men had finished unloading their tanks from trains in Lvov, and the following day they moved forward into action. The weather was terrible, with a thaw one day followed by heavy snow the next. For the first day of the operation, the Army 506th Heavy Panzer Battalion took the lead with its Tiger Is battering away through a large pak-front of antitank guns. Now the Frundsberg Division took over the advance for the final 32km (20 miles) to Hube's men. It then immediately ran into a concealed pak-front, and so the division's reconnaissance unit was sent forward to pin-point the enemy gun pit and bunker positions. Panzers were then brought up to blast the enemy antitank guns one-by-one. Soon the tanks were rolling eastwards again, with the divisional commander, SS-Gruppenführer Karl von Treuenfeld, leading the advance with the first panzer company. He decided that the link-up could be achieved sooner if a direct route across country was taken. At first the move looked like a typical daring Waffen-SS tactic, but within the space of a couple of hours Treuenfeld's tanks were strung out across several kilometres of muddy quagmire. The Waffen-SS general managed to get through to Hube's 6th Panzer Division with five tanks, but he was soon cut off from his division by a massive Soviet infantry attack. The Waffen-SS tank crews often had to fight dismounted from their bogged-down panzers to deal with Soviet tank-hunting squads that lurked in the woods and forests along the column's route. Bittrich came forward to sort out the mess. He organized the destruction of another pak-front, and the advance continued. By 6 April Bittrich had cleared the Soviet infantry brigades in the woods around

KESSEL BATTLES

the town of Buchach, which was the objective of Hube's columns. A supply column with 610 tonnes (600 tons) of fuel then moved down the corridor to refuel Hube's tanks and trucks, which were almost running on vapour alone. Over the next three days all the trapped German divisions were able to pass safely into the area held by II SS Panzer Corps. The rescue operation was a major success for Manstein, but the Führer saw it entirely differently. "Wars are not won with brilliantly organized retreats," ranted Hitler. The "saviour of the Eastern Front" was relieved and replaced by Field Marshal Walter Model, who had a reputation for issuing "fight to the last man and bullet" orders. Model was a tactician much more to Hitler's liking.

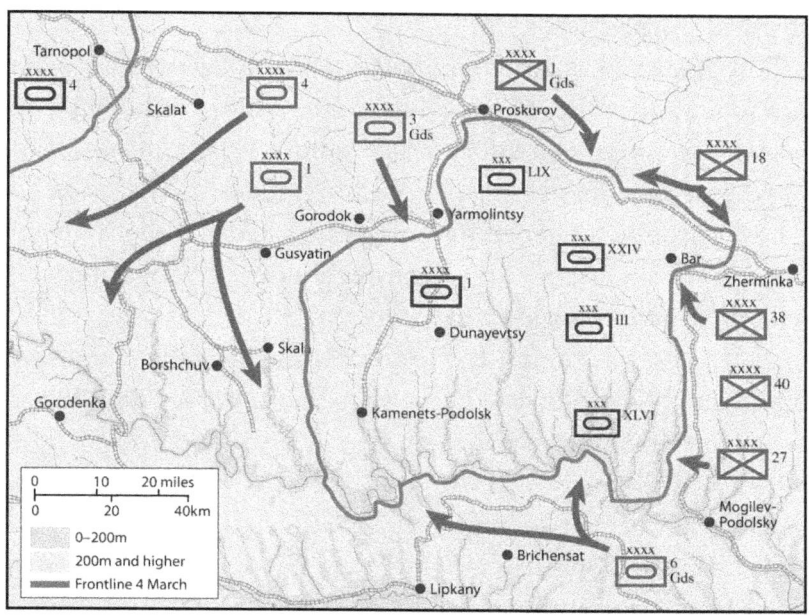

The Kamenets-Podolsk Pocket: Situation on 4 March 1944

Attention now turned to tidying up the new frontline, where dozens of small German detachments had been cut off. On 11 April, the Hohenstaufen Division was ordered to spearhead the rescue of 4000 Germans trapped in Ternopol. The operation was far from a success. On the first day the division got stuck in another quagmire, and then ran into heavy Soviet resistance. Model was far from impressed by the military professionalism of the Waffen-SS staff officers running the rescue mission, and ordered the division's panzer regiment to be placed under the command of an experienced army officer. The attack got moving again and pushed to within 8km (five miles) of the trapped troops. This time the Soviet ring held. The garrison attempted to break out but was massacred in the process. Only 53 men made it through to the Waffen-SS's lines.

The desperate state of the Eastern Front meant that even the remnants of the *Wiking* Division were mustered to fight in support of the rescue effort. Many soldiers still did not even have personal small arms after losing them in the Korsun/Cherkassy Pocket. Fortunately, the division had just been augmented by a fresh armoured regiment with 79 Panthers, which had been forming in Germany since December 1943. The division was committed to an operation to relieve the cut-off town of Kowel on the Ukrainian-Polish border, which had been surrounded by a Soviet spearhead since mid-March. The attack was ill-fated from the start, with *Wiking's* ammunition supply train being blown up by an artillery shell.

Wiking's no-nonsense commander, Gille, soon got a grip on the situation and personally led an assault force through the Soviet lines to break the siege. For several days he was trapped in the city, after a Russian counterattack severed the Waffen-SS corridor. Gille's men fought furiously to reopen a link to their commander, and the trapped garrison was finally relieved on 6 April. It was a victory of sorts, but the division had suffered many casualties, not just killed but also wounded, which meant the loss of veterans to hospitals and dressing stations. Replacements, if they were available at all, were poor by comparison.

On the southern wing of Army Group South, the *Totenkopf* Division was fighting a desperate rearguard battle around Kirovograd as the Eighth Army fell back to the River Dniester. In a move to pre-empt Soviet spearheads from seizing vital bridges on the German escape route into Romania, the *Totenkopf* Division was ordered to move back from the front to set up a new defensive line in the Eighth Army's rear communications zone. The urgency of the situation meant that Waffen-SS divisions' combat units were loaded into Me 232 Giant transport aircraft and flown on 11 March to their new positions. As the Eighth Army fell back in some disarray, many of its divisions passed through the *Totenkopf*'s lines. However, the Soviet advance soon forced the latter back, too. For most of April, it fell back into Romania and on several occasions had to fight desperate actions to avoid being trapped in pockets.

By May 1944, the Ukraine, which the Führer had been desperate to hold on to no matter what the cost, had been cleared of German forces, and within a few days the Crimea had also fallen. A succession of massive Soviet offensives had literally smashed their way through Manstein's Army Group South.

Throughout these offensives the Waffen-SS panzer divisions were in the thick of the action. They mounted counterattack after counterattack in the face of overwhelming odds, until they were down to almost their last tanks. In the end, though, Waffen-SS *élan* could not compensate for overwhelming superiority in both tanks and artillery. Ultimate defeat now seemed inevitable.

Chapter 9
HOLDING THE LINE

The Totenkopf *and* Wiking *Divisions in Poland, 1944.*

To throw back the Allied invasion of Normandy in June 1944, Adolf Hitler massed five Waffen-SS panzer divisions in France. Their battles with the American, British and Canadian armies are now well known, and have often overshadowed the desperate rearguard actions fought on the Eastern Front by the *Totenkopf* and *Wiking* Divisions to hold back the largest Soviet summer offensive of the war.

On 22 June 1944, the Soviet High Command unleashed Operation Bagration. In two weeks, the Wehrmacht's Army Group Centre was dissected with almost surgical precision by

Soviet pincer moves that lanced into its flanks and then chopped the weakened German forces into a series of pockets. By the first week of July, Soviet tanks were on the borders of Poland and a column of more than 100,000 German prisoners was paraded through the streets of Moscow. The battle destroyed 28 German divisions and 350,000 German soldiers were either killed or captured, including 47 generals. The destruction of Army Group Centre was the biggest ever defeat in German military history.

Almost overnight, a third of the German Eastern Front had ceased to exist. Desperate measures were needed to restore the situation. Hitler turned to Field Marshal Walter Model – his master of last-ditch defence – to save the day. Soon, he would turn to the only two Waffen-SS panzer divisions then available on the Eastern Front. They would be at the centre of his efforts to form a new defence line.

The remnants of the *Leibstandarte* and *Das Reich* Divisions were immediately shipped westwards after they escaped from the Kamenets Podolsk Pocket in April, to be rebuilt to meet the Anglo-American cross-Channel invasion. A few weeks later, the two divisions of II SS Panzer Corps followed them to France, leaving only the *Totenkopf* and *Wiking* Divisions in Romania and Poland respectively. In the brief spring lull, the two divisions were pulled out of the line to be rebuilt and re-equipped.

Wiking spent most of May and early June hunting partisans in the forests of eastern Poland. New tanks, trucks, artillery and weapons steadily arrived to bring it back up to something like a respectable strength by the end of June. In March, its Panther battalion was diverted to take part in Operation Margarethe to occupy Hungary and depose its government that was threatening to defect to the Allied cause. The operation went smoothly, and

HOLDING THE LINE

Wiking's panzer crews were not involved in any action, but the whole business showed just how precarious the situation on the Eastern Front was for the Third Reich at this stage of the war. The *Totenkopf* Division also received more than 6000 replacements from other Waffen-SS units and the concentration camp organization. Its most prized new asset was the return of its panzer regiment's 1st Battalion, with 79 new Panther tanks. The battalion had been training on the new tanks in Germany for several months, and it would significantly enhance the division's strike power. Heinrich Himmler, head of the SS organization, regarded the *Totenkopf* as his pet Waffen-SS division because of its links with the concentration camp branch of his empire, and he took a great interest in making sure it was properly equipped.

The Reichsführer-SS also regarded the Eastern Front as far more important than the battles with the Western Allies. The struggle with Stalin's Communist Soviet Union was at the heart of Nazi ideology, and Himmler wanted to ensure his Waffen-SS troops had all the tools necessary to pursue the campaign in the East through to final victory.

As well as rebuilding the *Totenkopf* and *Wiking* Divisions, plans were made to send another SS panzer corps to the Eastern Front to lead the two divisions. IV SS Panzer Corps was formed in 1943 to train Waffen-SS forces in western Europe, and would eventually be committed to action in Poland in August 1944, under the command of the veteran SS-Obergruppenführer Herbert Gille. This corps was intended to fight mobile battles, unlike III SS Panzer Corps, which spent the whole of the war in the northern sector of the Eastern Front leading a rag-tag collection of Waffen-SS infantry units.

As Operation Bagration gathered momentum and the German front began to crumble, the call went out for reserves to try to form breakwaters in the face of the tidal wave of Soviet tanks. On 25 June the *Totenkopf* Division was alerted for a move north, and it started to prepare its vehicles for loading onto trains. The Russian offensive had thrown the German rail network into confusion, though, and it took the trains carrying the *Totenkopf* two weeks to get to the scene of the action: northeastern Poland. The division was ordered to form a defence line near the Polish city of Grodno and to provide a safe haven for the remnants of the German Fourth Army, which were fleeing west ahead of the Russian advance.

The roads into the town were clogged with huge convoys of German soldiers and civilian refugees. Close on their heels were Soviet armoured columns, complete with tank-riding infantry to secure any gains. More than 400 tanks were soon thrown against the *Totenkopf*'s rearguard. It held them off for 11 days, until the division was ordered to fall back towards Warsaw. At this point the Luftwaffe's *Hermann Göring* Panzer Division moved up to support the *Totenkopf*, and for almost a week the two divisions held Siedlce, 80km (50 miles) east of Warsaw, in the face of attacks by the Soviet Second Tank Army. (the German panzer units had arrived at the key road and rail junction on 24 July, only hours ahead of the Soviet XI Tank Corps). Luftwaffe Stuka dive-bombers also provided support in these battles.

In six days of heavy street fighting, the Germans held off the Soviet armour spearheaded by XI Tank Corps. To finally clear out the elite German units, the Russians had to bring up batteries of

Katyusha rocket launchers and launch raids by several wings of heavy bombers. As this battle was raging, on 27 July the Soviet High Command launched III and XVI Tank Corps, supported by VIII Guards Tank Corps, with a combined strength of some

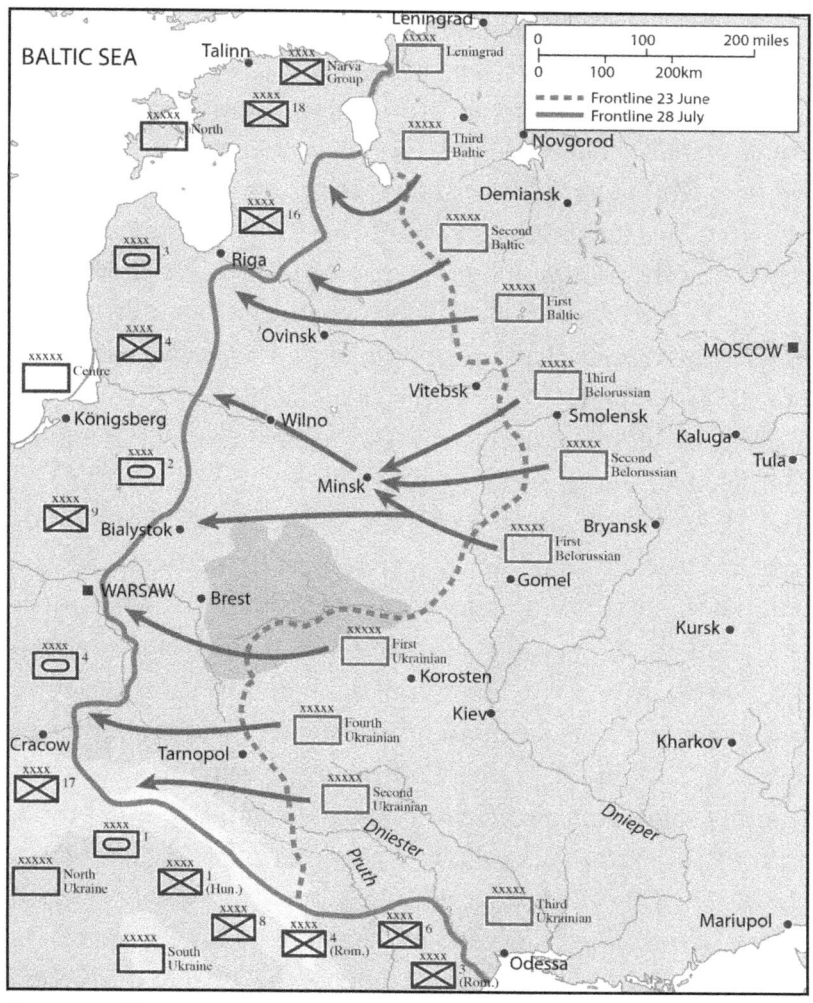

Operation Bagration: 23 June–28 July 1944

500 tanks, in a wide flanking movement to the south. This move caught the Germans by surprise, and two days later Soviet tanks had advanced 48km (30 miles) and were in the suburbs of the Polish capital, Warsaw.

Again, Model ordered his panzer divisions to race back to head off the Soviet spearheads. The *Totenkopf* and *Hermann Goring* Divisions, now joined by *Wiking*, were launched into a desperate counterattack to drive back the Soviet spearheads from the River Vistula. The *Wiking* Division had arrived by train in western Warsaw on 27 July, and moved through the city to take up defensive positions to hold off the Russians. The city was tense after its citizens had been ordered to mobilize themselves to repel the "Red menace". Civilian labour groups were forced to build improvised defences. The citizens of Warsaw, however, had other ideas. After almost five years of brutal Nazi occupation, the appearance of Soviet tanks a few kilometres to the east signalled that freedom was at hand.

On 1 August, the freedom fighters of the Polish Home Army rose in rebellion. All over the city guerrilla fighters attacked German-held buildings and started to fortify 'liberated' zones in the city and along the western bank of the Vistula, which cut Warsaw in two. In a matter of days most of the city centre had been cleared of German units. Isolated German positions were quickly seized by the Polish forces, using a mixture of captured and improvised weapons. The fighting was brutal, with little quarter being shown by either side, and soon one of the biggest street battles in military history was about to reach its tragic end. The Polish leaders depended on the swift arrival of Soviet tanks on the western side of the Vistula. However, the Home Army had failed to read the flow of the battle on the eastern bank of the Vistula between the Germans and the Soviet Second Tank Army.

As Soviet tanks cautiously entered Praga during the morning of 31 July, the eastern suburb of Warsaw, the prospects for an early liberation of Poland's capital seemed high. Unknown to the Russians, they were about to encounter a whirlwind. The *Totenkopf*, *Wiking* and *Hermann Göring* Divisions were attacking, as well as two army panzer divisions. The German panzers moved southwards into the flanks of the Russian tank columns. All day the battle raged, with German Panthers knocking out scores of Russian T-34s. German troops worked their way around the flanks of the Soviet III Tank Corps. The latter's troops, tired after almost six weeks of constant fighting, could put up little resistance. The corps only just managed to escape the German pincers, and by the end of the day the Soviets had been evicted from Praga. The attack was decisive and sealed the fate of the Warsaw Rising, even before it had begun. With the Germans now entrenched in Praga in strength, there was now no hope that the Russians would be easily able to link up with the Polish Home Army.

The Soviets now tried a wide encircling move to the north of Warsaw. By 4 August IV SS Panzer Corps, now with the *Totenkopf* and *Wiking* Divisions under its command, had already been ordered by Model to set up a blocking position north of the city, and was ready and waiting when the Soviet storm burst on 14 August. For a week the Waffen-SS formation held off 15 Russian infantry divisions and two tank corps. Human-wave attacks were repulsed on a daily basis, with thousands of Russian troops being killed in front of the German lines. The Soviets now poured in extra infantry divisions and hundreds more tanks. Heavy attacks, supported by hundreds of Stormovik fighter-bombers, added to the pounding, and by 26 August the *Totenkopf* had to fall back towards Praga under the deluge of firepower. A Waffen-SS counterattack on 11 September drove the Soviets back, and again defeated a link-up with the Polish Home Army.

The *Totenkopf* and *Wiking* Divisions were the linchpins of the German operation to crush the Warsaw Rising, even though they did not actually take part in the fighting against the Polish Home Army. By preventing a link-up with the Red Army, they consigned the population of the city to two months of siege. Hitler was infuriated that the Poles, whom he classed "subhumans", had dared to challenge German rule. They would pay for their defiance. The massive 600mm Karl mortar was brought up to blast whole city blocks.

On 2 August SS-Obergruppenführer Erich von dem Bach-Zelewski was appointed to put down the rising – no matter what it took. Civilians and prisoners were indiscriminately butchered by Bach-Zelewski's SS special police squads and Sonderkommando, who systematically moved through the city, 'eliminating' pockets of resistance. On 2 October, the Poles – starving, with their ammunition supplies exhausted and all hopes of rescue by the Red Army extinguished – came out waving white flags. Hitler ordered that all of the city's population be deported. Many of them ended up in SS death camps. The Führer then ordered that the city was to be levelled. For almost three months, German demolition squads turned Warsaw into the world's largest pile of rubble.

IV SS Panzer Corps, flush with victory, remained on duty in northeastern Poland for the rest of 1944, where it tried to hold

HOLDING THE LINE

the line against repeated Soviet offensives that started on 10 October. It had to fall back at the end of that month, but the front soon stabilized as the Russian drive ran out of momentum once more.

The Soviet High Command was now preoccupied with clearing out the Balkans. Russian troops swept through Romania, Yugoslavia, Bulgaria and up to the borders of Hungary. In October 1944 the Hungarians were wavering, so Hitler ordered the launching of Operation Panzerfaust to seize key points throughout the country's capital, Budapest. Adolf Hitler's daring Waffen-SS commando leader, Otto Skorzeny, led a raid to seize Hungarian government leaders. Other SS and army units then occupied the city and prepared it for defence. At this period Soviet troops were only a few kilometres from Budapest, and by Christmas the city would be encircled. When that happened some 70,000 German troops would be trapped.

The combat performance of the Waffen-SS divisions was the only bright spot in a gloomy strategic situation on the Eastern Front. The *Totenkopf* Division, for example, had performed consistently well and had been noted in the diary of the Ninth Army on numerous occasions. Its heroics did not escape Hitler, who remarked about the Death's Head Division: "whenever one sent them reinforcements [they] always counterattacked successfully."

Yet not even the *Totenkopf* Division could stop the masses of enemy tanks. The comments of panzer commander Martin Steiger, Panzer Regiment 3, are indicative of the problems faced by the Germans at this stage of the war. Talking of the fighting around Warsaw he stated: "Enemy tanks, growing in numbers like flies, broke through, destroyed supply units and kept fighting well behind our lines. We were thrown at them, knocked them out and lost some more of our panzers in the process. When we returned again to where our main frontline had been only the day before when we left it, we found it captured already by the Russians. This happened almost every day. The losses of men and panzers were staggering.'

At the end of 1944, the Eastern Front had been pushed back to the borders of Germany itself. Soviet troops were poised to strike at the very heart of the Third Reich. The five Waffen-SS panzer divisions that had been committed to the ill-fated Ardennes Offensive in the West in December 1944 were ordered to regroup, and prepared to move east for their final battle with the Red Army.

Chapter 10
SPRING AWAKENING

The failure of the Sixth SS Panzer Army in Hungary.

In his Berlin bunker in February 1945, an all-out offensive led by six Waffen-SS panzer divisions to secure Hungary's oil fields seemed very logical to Adolf Hitler. Almost to a man, however, the Führer's generals thought it was madness. Huge Soviet armies were at this time on the eastern bank of the River Oder, less than 160km (100 miles) from Berlin itself. The Third Reich's elite armoured forces were needed for the last-ditch battle to defend its capital from the Russians, or so it seemed to General Heinz Guderian, the penultimate chief of staff of the German Army. The father of Germany's panzer elite could only shrug his shoulders and pass on the lunatic orders of his Führer. Hitler was now a nervous wreck, who could only keep going with the aid of drugs prescribed by his equally insane personal doctor, Theodor Morell. The Führer was reduced to moving flags around the map table in his bunker. The flags no longer represented armies or divisions, merely ghost units with no equipment or ammunition and even less will to fight. It was as if the Führer did not want to hear the bad news that his Thousand Year Reich only had a few weeks left, before it would be erased from the map for good.

The Waffen-SS panzer divisions started concentrating in Hungary in December 1944, after a Soviet offensive had pushed deep into the country and surrounded its capital, Budapest. SS-Obergruppenführer Karl von Pfeffer-Wildrenbruch and a combined force of 70,000 German and Hungarian troops were trapped in the city. What followed was depressingly predictable: a rescue force was organized; after it fought its way to within a few kilometres of the trapped garrison, Hitler refused to allow it to break out. In the end only a few hundred men were able to escape from the city.

By Christmas Day 1944, the city was surrounded. In response, Hitler ordered IV SS Panzer Corps to be moved from Poland to spearhead the rescue mission with the *Totenkopf* and *Wiking* Divisions. SS-Obergruppenführer Herbert Gille's men spent four days on freezing trains moving down to Komorno on the River Danube. They unloaded their 100 tanks and headed east to intercept Russian spearheads advancing westwards along the south bank of the Danube. Operation Konrad got under way with a night attack on New Year's Day, which initially caught the Soviet XXXI Rifle Corps by surprise. The

Waffen-SS Panthers and Panzer IVs crashed through the unprepared Russians and drove eastwards for almost 48km (30 miles), knocking out 200 enemy tanks as they did so.

Failure before Budapest

The *Totenkopf* Division advanced directly eastwards on the left flank, along the banks of the Danube, while the *Wiking* Division moved southeastwards directly towards Budapest. When the *Totenkopf* hit a strong pak-front, it too turned southwards to join *Wiking*'s push. Lacking the strength to batter his way past Soviet defences, Gille used his veteran troops to try to dodge past Soviet strong-points and find a way through to Budapest. With the route south blocked, he sent *Wiking*'s Westland Panzergrenadier Regiment on a march deep behind enemy lines after it found a route over the Vertes Mountains. With the Soviets now alerted to the German intentions, though, it was not long before they moved reinforcements up to close off the northern route into the Hungarian capital.

On 12 January 1945, the Waffen-SS troops pulled back from the front and disappeared into the forests along the Danube. The Soviets were convinced they had seen off the German attack. They had no idea that Gille's troops were in fact moving south to open a new front. Six days later they burst out of the morning mist to smash into the Russian CXXXV Rifle Corps, which without tank support was an easy target for the Waffen-SS units. The German tanks rolled over its frontline positions on 18 January, and then started to shoot up its supply convoys and artillery positions. By the evening they had covered 32km (20 miles), brushing aside a counterattack by the weak Soviet VII Mechanized Corps. More Russian tanks were sent into action the following day, and they received the same treatment. The *Totenkopf*'s antitank battalion, deployed with the advance guard of the division's *Totenkopf* Panzergrenadier Regiment, was instrumental in breaking up several counterattacks by the Soviet XVIII Tank and CXXXIII Rifle Corps. Its new Panzerjäger IVs self-propelled guns were particularly effective. This heavily armoured version of the Panzer IV tank was equipped with the powerful L/70 75mm cannon, which was also used in the Panther tank. The Danube valley, with its open fields and small villages, was ideal tank country. The winter frost meant the ground was still hard, so Gille's handful of panzers was able to race forward across country. They crossed the Szarviz Canal in a night-time assault, and by the morning of 20 January German armour was on the banks of the Danube. Gille's men now motored northwards, cutting into the rear lines of communications of the Soviet Fifty-Seventh Army. The Red Army was in a panic. The Soviet commanders on the west bank of the Danube were convinced they would soon be surrounded by IV SS Panzer Corps and the German Army's 1st Panzer Division. On 24 January, the *Wiking* and *Totenkopf* Divisions surged forward again, inflicting heavy losses on the Soviet V Guards Cavalry and I Guards Mechanized Corps. They got to within 24km (15 miles) of Budapest before the arrival of the last Soviet reserves, XXIII Tank Corps, stopped them in their tracks. Gille's men attacked with great *élan*, and used their tried-and-tested infiltration tactics to take advantage of the weakened state of the Soviet infantry divisions around Budapest. Most Soviet infantry divisions and tank corps were reduced to less than 5000 men each, following several months of non-stop fighting through the Balkans. It appeared that victory for the Waffen-SS divisions was at hand.

SPRING AWAKENING

Three days later, 12 Soviet infantry divisions joined the tank corps in a major counterattack against the Waffen-SS divisions. The SS units held their ground, but Hitler now ordered IV SS Panzer Corps to fall back so it could regroup and join a major operation he was planning to defeat the entire Soviet army group in Hungary. Ignoring pleas from his generals that now was the moment to order a break-out from Budapest, Hitler refused to consider the idea. Budapest would be relieved by the Sixth SS Panzer Army. Therefore, there was no need for a break-out.

The situation reminded many German generals of Stalingrad two years before. Pfeffer-Wildrenbruch followed his Führer's orders to the letter. Hitler decorated him with the Knight's Cross for his bravery, but some thought the Führer was just trying to shame the Waffen-SS general into not surrendering. With Gille's men now falling back in the face of massive pressure, the Budapest garrison's position was becoming even more precarious. Now free from the need to deal with rampaging Waffen-SS panzers, the Soviets were able to concentrate all their efforts on eliminating Pfeffer-Wildrenbruch's hapless command. The Waffen-SS general proved to be particularly inept, allowing his main supply dump to be overrun. It was only a matter of time before Budapest went the same way as Stalingrad.

In January 1945, five Waffen-SS divisions were in the process of pulling out of Belgium after the failure of the Ardennes Offensive. Hitler wanted them concentrated to lead his offensive into Hungary, which he thought would turn the course of the war. He repeatedly told his generals that they did not understand that modern warfare was about the control of economic resources. A special order was issued by the head of the SS, Heinrich Himmler, for the divisions to be pulled back into Germany to be refitted for their new offensive. Almost the total production of Germany's shattered armaments industry was to be diverted to the SS divisions. In the skies over the Third Reich, British and American bombers were pounding Germany's factories and cities on an almost daily basis, while Russian tanks were rampaging through the Silesian industrial region. The efforts to re-equip the Waffen-SS divisions therefore stretched Germany's armaments industry to the limit. There were no more reserves left. The coming offensive would the last throw of the dice for Hitler's Third Reich.

Throughout January and into February 1945, new tanks, assault guns, halftracks, artillery and other equipment arrived by train at barracks and training grounds in central Germany. Thousands of raw recruits and drafted Luftwaffe and Kriegsmarine (German Navy) personnel, who no longer had aircraft or ships to serve in, found themselves impressed into the Waffen-SS. Crash training courses were organized to try to mould this raw material into an elite fighting force. The results were very mixed.

For the first time, six SS panzer divisions would be committed to an operation on the Eastern Front under the command of SS panzer corps, and two of those corps would be under the command of the Sixth SS Panzer Army. This army had been raised in September 1944 to lead the Waffen-SS panzer divisions in the Ardennes. Hitler's favourite Waffen-SS general, SS-Oberstgruppenführer Josef 'Sepp' Dietrich, remained in command of this army, even though he obviously did not relish such a high-level command. He left most of the day-to-day running of the army to his staff and concentrated on what he liked doing best: carrying out morale-boosting visits to frontline regiments. Dietrich loved being in the thick

SPRING AWAKENING

of the action, and relished organizing small squads of men for daredevil operations. Not surprisingly, therefore, many army generals – and some Waffen-SS ones as well – thought Dietrich had been promoted way beyond his ability. He just about coped as a divisional commander, but was out of his depth as a corps and army commander. The Führer would not have a word said against him, however, because of Dietrich's early work as Hitler's bodyguard in the 1920s.

There was great rivalry between the two corps in the Sixth SS Panzer Army. The most favoured formation was I SS Panzer Corps *Leibstandarte Adolf Hitler* led by SS-Gruppenführer Hermann Priess, the former commander of the *Totenkopf* Division. It boasted the *Leibstandarte* and *Hitlerjugend* Divisions (the latter was to see action on the Eastern Front for the first time during the coming offensive). The *Leibstandarte* Division's panzer regiment was reinforced with a full battalion of 36 of the new super-heavy Tiger II, or King Tiger, tanks. These 71.12-tonne (70-ton) monsters boasted frontal armour 250mm (9.84in) thick that was impervious to almost all antitank weapons then in service. However, they were notoriously mechanically unreliable, and more would be abandoned on the battlefields of Hungary following breakdowns than were lost to enemy fire. The 501st SS Heavy Panzer Battalion was one of three such units created by the Waffen-SS in the final months of the war, which used the Tiger II tank. These units grew out of the Tiger I companies that had served with the three original SS panzer divisions since 1943. The two other battalions, the 502nd and 503rd, were sent to the East Prussian and Berlin sectors in the final months of the war, and so missed the offensive in Hungary. The *Leibstandarte*'s other panzer battalion fielded 27 Panzer IV tanks, 41 Panthers and eight antiaircraft tanks. The latter were now essential to tank operations because of Allied air supremacy, which made it very risky for German tanks to move around in the open during daylight hours.

The *Hitlerjugend* Division could only muster one battalion for its panzer regiment, with 40 Panzer IVs and 44 Panthers. The division also had 20 of the new Jagdpanzer IV antitank self-propelled gun, plus more than 150 armoured halftracks. Also attached to the division was the 560th Heavy Anti-Tank Battalion, which fielded 31 Jagdpanzer IVs and 16 Jagdpanthers. This latter vehicle combined a Panther chassis with a fixed 88mm cannon.

A heavy punch was also packed by II SS Panzer Corps, under the command of SS-Gruppenführer Willi Bittrich, which contained the *Das Reich* and *Hohenstaufen* Divisions. Like I SS Panzer Corps, Bittrich's command had a heavy artillery regiment equipped with towed 210mm howitzers, and a rocket launcher regiment with Nebelwerfers to provide heavy fire support during assault operations.

Bittrich's panzer regiments were short of tanks, but the shortfall was made up with Sturmgeschütz (StuG) assault guns. They were distributed to the panzer regiments' second battalions to augment their Panzer IVs. The *Das Reich* Division boasted 34 Panthers, 19 Panzer IVs and 28 StuG IIIs, while the *Hohenstaufen* Division had 31 Panthers, 26 Panzer IVs and 25 StuG IIIs. The *Hohenstaufen*'s sister division, *Frundsberg*, had served in II SS Panzer Corps all through the Normandy campaign, at Arnhem and during the Ardennes Offensive, but in January 1945 it was detached and posted to the Vistula sector of the Eastern Front, taking with it its 38 Panzer IVs and

53 Panthers. It would not join the rest of the Sixth SS Panzer Army for the Hungary offensive.

Hitler was determined that the move of Dietrich's army to Hungary be kept secret, so he ordered the famous Waffen-SS general to move his headquarters to the Eastern Front via Berlin. There he made a number of high-profile visits to the front in an attempt to convince the Soviets that the Waffen-SS panzer reserve was about to be committed to the defence of Germany's capital. The *Leibstandarte*'s King Tigers were also shipped via the Reich's capital to add to the pretence. The chaotic state of Germany's rail network at this point in the war meant the exercise was fraught with risks, and the trains carrying the tanks

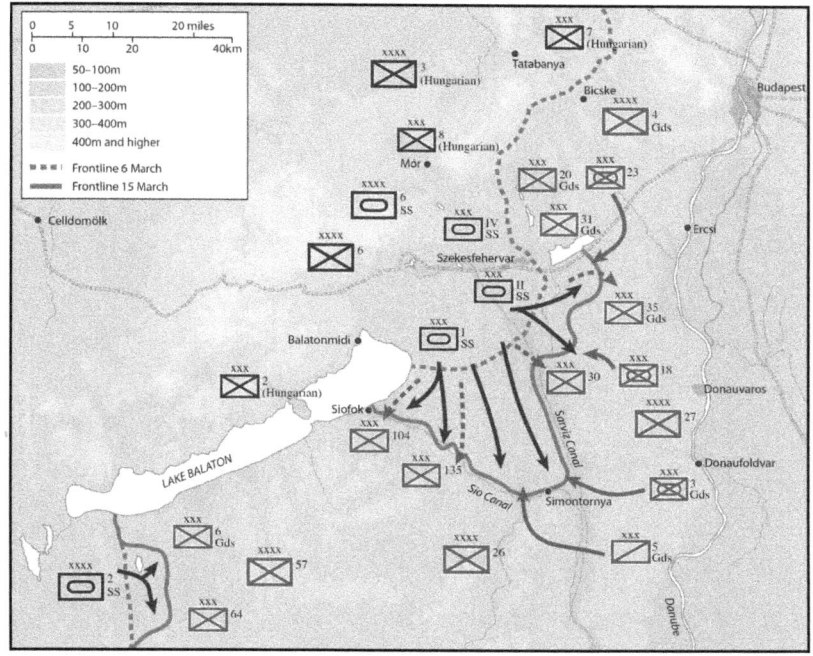

Operation Spring Awakening: 6–15 March 1945

were lucky to have escaped the attention of Allied bombers and make it to their start line in Hungary.

Operation Spring Awakening was envisaged by Hitler as a knock-out blow against Soviet forces in the Balkans. The initial phase of the assault would be a three-pronged pincer attack to trap and destroy the Russian troops on the west bank of the River Danube. German forces would then turn eastwards and free the trapped garrison in Budapest. There was then talk of the offensive continuing southwards to drive the Red Army out of the Balkans altogether and regain control of Romania's oil wells. However, the whole scheme was based on fantasy. For one thing,

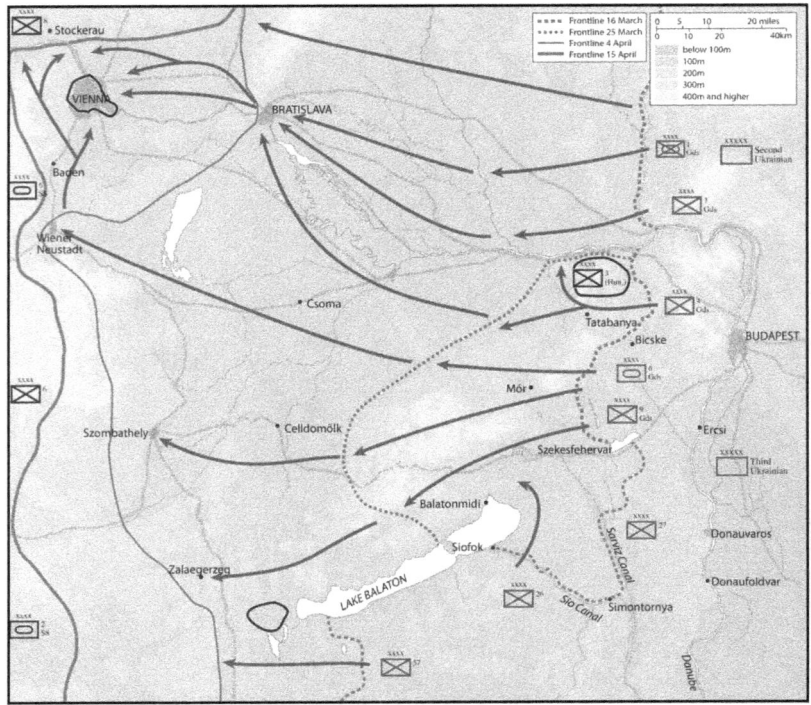

The Vienna Offensive: 16 March–15 April 1945

SPRING AWAKENING

Budapest was on the brink of falling even before Dietrich's troops had started their attack.

On 16 February, Pfeffer-Wildrenbruch led a breakout attempt at the head of the last 16,000 German troops in the city. They did not get very far before they were ambushed. The Waffen-SS general tried to escape through the sewers, only to emerge in the middle of a Soviet regiment and was captured. Only 785 Germans made it through the Soviet ring.

As the pitiful drama in Budapest was entering its final act, Dietrich's Sixth SS Panzer Army was at last arriving in Hungary in some strength. The German offensive would be conducted in two phases. It was to kick off with a preliminary operation, code-named South Wind, by I SS Panzer Corps to destroy the Soviet bridgehead on the western bank of the River Gran, which threatened the German left flank along the banks of the Danube. The Soviet bridgehead, held by seven infantry divisions and a number of armoured units, was to be bludgeoned out of existence by a head-on attack by the *Leibstandarte* and *Hitlerjugend* Divisions.

SS-Obersturmbannführer Joachim Peiper, commanding the *Leibstandarte*'s panzer kampfgruppe, was to lead the attack, which was channelled by a series of wide water courses into a narrow 16km (10-mile) frontage. The battlefield was criss-crossed by numerous canals, which were heavily defended by Russian antitank guns and dug-in T-34/85 tanks. The latter was the upgraded version of the famous Soviet tank, which now boasted an 85mm high-velocity cannon as its main armament. Peiper commanded all the *Leibstandarte*'s tanks, including its Tiger IIs, a battalion of panzergrenadiers riding in armoured halftracks, and a battalion of self-propelled artillery.

Army infantry units were initially committed to the battle during the evening of 16/17 February, after a corps fire mission by all the German guns facing the bridgehead. The attack achieved surprise, and the infantrymen were at first able to advance 8km (five miles) before they ran into the first enemy pak-front. Peiper ordered his King Tigers to motor to their assistance. When the heavy tanks rolled into the range of the Russian antitank guns, they started attracting heavy fire from the 76mm cannons. The shells just bounced off the front of the King Tigers, however, allowing the German tanks to destroy all the Soviet guns blocking the advance.

By evening, the *Leibstandarte* and Hitlerjugend Divisions were at Parizs Canal and making plans to expand the small bridgeheads they had seized. Hitlerjugend combat engineers built a bridge capable of bearing Panzer IV and Panther tanks, to allow them push another 16km (10 miles) into the bridgehead. During the day the Russians mounted repeated small-scale attacks against the Waffen-SS incursion, inflicting casualties and delaying the advance. Armoured kampfgruppen from both divisions advanced on 19 February, employing panzerkeil tactics. With the heavy King Tigers and Panthers in the lead, any Soviet tanks or antitank guns that tried to block the German advance were quickly silenced by the panzers' devastating firepower. By early afternoon the Waffen-SS tank crews were at the Danube, in the eastern bottom corner of the bridgehead.

The next day, the armoured spearhead was ordered to swing north to deal with the Soviet IV Guards Mechanized Corps that was still entrenched on the west bank of the Gran. Peiper decided that the attack should go in during darkness to protect the assault group of Panzer IV tanks from a huge Soviet artillery position on the east bank of the Gran. The panzers rolled into action with flares and burning tanks illuminating the battlefield. Several German tanks were lost, but the route north was opened. The *Leibstandarte* Division now halted its tanks to refuel and rearm. The Hitlerjugend's 25th Panzergrenadier Regiment was then ordered into action against the northern flank of the IV Guards Corps' bridgehead. Attacking southwards during the evening of 22/23 February, the combined panzer-infantry operation degenerated into confusion when German units failed to recognize each other in the darkness and started trading fire. This attracted Russian artillery fire, and the assault was stalled in no-man's land for several hours. Then the assault tanks got stuck in a minefield, losing several vehicles. Only a daring flank attack by the division's armoured personnel carrier battalion saved the day. By chance it found a route around the minefield, and was soon inside a village full of T-34 tanks. The panzergrenadiers dismounted and stalked the Russian tanks though the village with Panzerschreck hand-held antitank rocket launchers. With no infantry to protect them, the Russian tanks were soon fleeing from the village. This opened the way for the rest of the division to move through a path in the minefield, and clear the remaining Russian positions.

After a day recovering from this carnage, I SS Panzer Corps spent 23 February preparing for the final assault on the Soviet bridgehead. The two Waffen-SS divisions staged a concentric night attack, with King Tigers and Panthers leading the way. In only six hours of heavy fighting the position was cleared, and the Russians eventually withdrew, blowing up the last bridge across the Gran at 08:30 hours on 24 February. They left a trail of destroyed and abandoned equipment behind them. More than

2000 Russians had been killed, a further 6000 wounded and 500 captured by I SS Panzer Corps. Some 71 tanks and 180 artillery pieces were also lost in the week-long battle. The Waffen-SS paid a heavy price for the victory, though, losing almost 3000 casualties and a dozen tanks destroyed. Scores more tanks were badly damaged, and had to be pulled back from the panzer regiments for urgent repairs. Some of the manpower losses were replaced with more half-trained draftees from the Luftwaffe, indicating the low quality of the personnel now available to the Waffen-SS.

With the Gran bridgehead eliminated, Hitler was able to order Operation Spring Awakening to roll forward to the south. Some 400,000 German troops, supported by 7000 artillery pieces, 965 Luftwaffe combat aircraft, and 400 tanks and self-propelled guns were to attack on 6 March. The *schwerpunkt*, or main effort, of the operation was between Lakes Balaton and Valencei, with the Sixth SS Panzer Army leading. It had the bulk of the German armour under its command. Gille's IV SS Panzer Corps was to support the operation on the left flank of Dietrich's army. For the first time, six Waffen-SS panzer divisions would roll into battle together. Not surprisingly, the Führer was very optimistic about Spring Awakening's prospects. In Hungary, though, the Waffen-SS commanders were far from optimistic about the coming battle. They were expected to advance over waterlogged terrain, which was dissected by numerous rivers and canals. Of greater concern was the fact that the Russians knew they were coming.

In the month since Gille's panzers had attacked, the approaches to Budapest were now protected by heavily dug-in antitank tank guns and infantry positions. To the south of the city, where Dietrich's attack was to be made, the Soviets based their defensive plans on the network of canals that ran across the flat plain. The start of the spring thaw also worked in the defenders' favour, because it made movement off road by any type of vehicle, even tracked ones, almost impossible. Some 16 Russian rifle divisions were in the path of Dietrich's panzers, with two tank corps and two mechanized corps, with some 150 tanks, in direct support just behind the frontline southwest of Lake Balaton itself.

More ominously for the Third Reich, the Soviets were building up their armoured forces north of Budapest for their own offensive along the Danube valley – the Sixth SS Panzer Army would attack into the jaws of an overwhelming Soviet armada of more than 1000 tanks. The attack plan called for I SS Panzer Corps to advance southwards to link up with the Second Panzer Army advancing northwards. II SS Panzer Corps was to move directly eastwards towards the Danube, to protect the right flank of the Waffen-SS attack.

Operation Spring Awakening began officially at 04:30 hours on 6 March, with a massive barrage from the artillery of the Sixth SS Panzer Army. First to move forward were the panzergrenadiers of the *Leibstandarte*, whose first task was to open several lanes through a Russian minefield before they could begin clearing an extensive system of trenches and strong-points at bayonet point. This took all the morning, and then the division's panzer kampfgruppe was able to race forward. After a few kilometres, though, it ran into a well-prepared pak-front, protected by more minefields. As the kampfgruppe's tanks and armoured halftracks tried to deploy off the roads to engage the enemy antitank guns, they started to get stuck in axle-deep mud. The panzergrenadiers had to press home their attacks without armoured support. Not surprisingly, the rate of advance was unimpressive.

Advancing on the *Leibstandarte*'s left, the *Hitlerjugend* Division found the going equally hard. Its tanks also got stuck in the mud, and the division was only able to push 1.6km (one mile) forward. II SS Panzer Corps' attack did not even reach its assembly area until well after dark.

Thanks to their successful initial defence, the Russians were able to deploy an extra infantry corps, with limited tank support, across the path of I SS Panzer Corps. They did not move their main armoured reserves, but kept them around Budapest in preparation for their own offensive.

On 7 March the German attack began to gather momentum, as both the *Leibstandarte* and *Hitlerjugend* Divisions at last broke through the Soviet defences and were able to launch their panzer kampfgruppen into action to exploit the breaches created by the panzergrenadiers. During the night, the Soviet infantry divisions began a deliberate withdrawal back to the Sio Canal, where a new defensive front was being prepared by the reserve divisions. II Panzer Corps' attack did not get very far before it ground to a halt in waterlogged ground. One tank even sank up to its turret ring in the mud!

As dawn broke on 8 March, German fortunes looked as if they had changed. The *Hitlerjugend* surged 16km (10 miles) forward until it ran into a pak-front dug-in on ridge lines. The division's reconnaissance battalion was ordered to take the position in a night attack, to allow the advance to begin again at first light. A dozen Jagdpanthers and Jagdpanzer IVs formed a panzerkeil which charged up the hill and routed the defenders. The reconnaissance battalion's halftracks followed close behind, and the Waffen-SS troopers machine-gunned and grenaded the fleeing Russian troops as they drove among them.

Bittrich's men, spearheaded by *Das Reich*, now ran headlong into the Soviet XXX Corps and XVIII Tank Corps, which battled furiously to hold them back from the Danube. The Russians even resorted to using their heavy antiaircraft artillery in the direct-fire mode against German tanks. The next day the *Hohenstaufen* and *Wiking* Divisions joined the attack, driving a wedge 24km (15 miles) into the Soviet line.

I SS Panzer Corps now caught up with the retreating Russians on the Sio Canal, with German Panthers and Jagdpanthers inflicting heavy losses on a number of Soviet truck convoys that had not yet crossed over the canal.

For the next two days, *Leibstandarte* and *Hitlerjugend* panzergrenadiers battled to cross the Sio Canal. Small Russian rearguard detachments had to be evicted, one-by-one, from a series of villages on the north bank of the canal. King Tigers were brought up to deal with the Soviet antitank guns and Su-100 assault guns that were left behind to slow up the German advance. Heavy rain and sleet made this miserable work, and scores of vehicles got stuck in mud as they tried to manoeuvre through the fields along the canal bank. Soviet Stormovik fighter-bombers then appeared over the battlefield, and picked off many of the immobilized German tanks.

II SS Panzer Corps also kept battering its way forward, albeit at a snail's pace, with *Das Reich's* panzer regiments having a good day knocking out scores of Soviet tanks. To pen in this incursion, the Soviet XXIII Tank Corps was thrown into the battle against the Waffen-SS division.

The fighting along the Sio Canal reached a climax on 12 March with a major effort being mounted to push bridgeheads across the 30m- (98ft-) wide obstacle. The *Hitlerjugend's* attack ended in slaughter, when its fire-support panzers and Jagdpanzers were forced to fall back from the canal bank by a withering barrage of antitank gun fire. The panzergrenadiers pressed on, only to be machine-gunned in their rubber assaults boats as they tried to row across the canal. A few of them made it across and established a precarious bridgehead. In the *Leibstandarte*'s sector, the attack fared better because the division was able to bring its troops forward through a town and protect them from enemy fire until the last moment, before they too rushed across the canal. Deadly 88mm flak guns were brought up to support the assault and, along with the King Tigers, they were able to neutralize many of the Soviet antitank guns and machine-gun bunkers. This firepower was enough to allow the establishment of a bridgehead during the night, and soon the division's combat engineers were at work erecting a tank bridge. A Jagdpanzer IV got over the structure, but the weight of a second vehicle was too much and the bridge collapsed into the water. Constant repairs were needed to keep it open to allow reinforcements to cross. They were desperately needed to deal with a counterattack by a regiment of T-34/85 tanks.

I SS Panzer Corps managed to hold onto its bridgeheads for three more days in the face of incessant Soviet counterattacks. Battalions, then regiments, were fed into the battle by the Soviets to keep the Waffen-SS penned in. The Red Army was winning the battle of attrition.

With his route south effectively blocked, Dietrich decided on 15 March to switch the *schwerpunkt* of his army away from I SS Panzer Corps to Bittrich's front. The *Leibstandarte* and *Hitlerjugend* were ordered to disengage and move north, before joining the attack towards the Danube.

The following day, however, the Soviets began their own offensive, which rendered Dietrich's orders irrelevant. More than 3000 vehicles, including 600 tanks, poured past Budapest and swept around both sides of Lake Valencei. Gille's IV SS Panzer Corps was engulfed in the storm, with the *Wiking* Division all but surrounded after a Hungarian division collapsed on its flank. Hitler issued orders that the division was to hold at all costs. The division's commander, SS-Oberführer Karl Ullrich, ignored the orders and pulled his troops back before they were trapped. The *Hohenstaufen* Division came to its rescue, also in defiance of the Führer's orders.

Bittrich and Gille now joined forces to hold open an escape route for I SS Panzer Corps, which was pulling back north as fast as it could to avoid encirclement. It managed to get out of the trap, but had to leave most of its damaged and bogged-in vehicles behind. By 20 March 1945, I SS Panzer Corps could only muster 80 tanks, assault guns and self-propelled guns fit for service. The remainder of Dietrich's army now mustered fewer than 100 tanks and assault guns. All the Waffen-SS divisions had suffered grievously during Spring Awakening, and most were below 50 percent strength and there was little prospect of any reinforcements to replace losses.

The German front in Hungary was shattered wide open by the Soviet offensive. It was never re-established. Dietrich's army started to fall back to Austria in the hope of defending the capital, Vienna. The Waffen-SS divisions were now constantly retreating, though every so often a handful of tanks and panzergrenadiers would turn to form a rearguard. Even these determined fighters were soon outflanked however, and the retreat would begin again.

When news reached Hitler's bunker about the retreat of the Waffen-SS, the Führer flew into a rage. The failure of his precious SS divisions was all the more hard to bear due to the faith he had previously had in their ability and Nazi ideological zeal. He sent a signal to Dietrich ordering the soldiers of the Sixth SS Panzer Army to remove their honorific Nazi armbands. In his eyes, they were no longer fit to wear the Führer's name on their uniforms.

The effect on the morale of the Waffen-SS divisions in Austria was catastrophic. Senior commanders ripped off their medals in disgust and ordinary grenadiers started to desert in large numbers. The men of Dietrich's army could see that the war was lost. Now, therefore, the main priority was to escape to the west to surrender to the Americans, and thus avoid the inevitable retribution at the hands of the soldiers of the triumphant Red Army.

Chapter 11
THE BITTER END

The end of the war and the verdict on the Waffen-SS.

On 24 April 1945, Adolf Hitler committed suicide in the ruins of Berlin. His Thousand Year Reich was in the process of being dismembered by the victorious allies. The Führer's chosen successor, Admiral Karl Dönitz, immediately began negotiations with the Allies concerning surrender.

Escaping from the Soviets was now the main priority of the seven Waffen-SS panzer divisions. These once-proud and arrogant units were now desperate to avoid falling into the hands of their vengeful enemies. In nearly four years of combat on the Eastern Front, the Waffen-SS men had learned from bitter experience that they could expect little mercy from the Red Army. Time and again, Waffen-SS prisoners, particularly officers, had been summarily executed by their communist captors. The Russians, however, were only behaving in the same way as the Waffen-SS had treated captured Soviet soldiers on numerous occasions.

The futile assault in Hungary and the subsequent Soviet offensive had reduced the Waffen-SS divisions to only a few thousand men each. The survivors were the hardcore veterans. Most of the draftees from recent months were dead, wounded or fleeing for home, their uniforms abandoned long ago.

Fittingly, two Waffen-SS panzer units had gone down fighting in the ruins of the Third Reich. The 502nd and 503rd Heavy Panzer Battalions had been diverted to the Berlin and East Prussian Fronts respectively in February 1945. Their King Tiger tanks inflicted heavy losses on the advancing Soviets, but the two battalions had been annihilated in the final battles in April.

The Waffen-SS panzer divisions were all in Czechoslovakia or Austria in the first week of May. German military power had collapsed. Partisans and citizens groups had seized control in many places, and they were anxiously waiting for either the Americans or Russians to arrive. German units were reduced to the status of roving bands of scavengers, moving from town to town trying to find supplies and shelter before moving on westwards. Occasionally they would turn on the Soviets and stage a brief rearguard action to ensure they could continue their march uninterrupted.

The *Leibstandarte* and *Das Reich* Divisions found themselves in central Czechoslovakia, amid an uprising against German rule. Their commanders negotiated a truce with the rebels and escorted several thousand German civilians out of Prague towards the advancing Americans. As they approached the American lines, the rump of the two divisions just melted away into small groups to try to find a way past the US Army outposts.

THE BITTER END

The *Frundsberg* Division was on the Czech-German border when the war ended and, rather than formally surrender, its officers and men split themselves up into small groups and headed for the American lines. A few made it, but most were trapped by Soviet patrols or killed by Czech partisans. Those captured by the Russians were shipped to Siberia, and only a handful returned home in 1955 when the Kremlin finally released its last batches of German prisoners.

In Austria, what was left of the *Hitlerjugend* Division surrendered en masse to the Americans under the watchful eye of a Russian tank column. At the last minute, the remaining 6000 *Hitlerjugend* troops stampeded past an American check-point rather than risk capture by the Russians. The *Hohenstaufen* Division was able to surrender peacefully to the American, while *Wiking* just broke up into small groups and disappeared into Austrian and Bavarian villages. Many of the staff officers of the various Waffen-SS panzer corps and the Sixth SS Panzer Army also took to the hills. American, British and French patrols soon arrested hundreds of Waffen-SS men as they tried to reach their home towns, or flee to Switzerland.

The *Totenkopf* Division suffered a tragic, or fitting depending on one's point of view, fate after an epic journey to the American lines. In spite of managing to cross into the American sector, the 3000 *Totenkopf* men were then handed over to the Russians. The senior officers were separated from the bulk of the men and executed by NKVD secret policemen. Hundreds of others were also executed as the remnants of the division were shipped to Stalin's Gulag in Siberia.

What was the legacy of the Waffen-SS panzer divisions? After six years of war, the Führer to whom they had promised blind obedience was dead and Germany was in ruins. More than a million men served in the Waffen-SS, and a third of them were killed in action. At the Nuremberg war crimes tribunal the SS – including the Waffen-SS – was declared a criminal organization, and its members stripped of the protection accorded by the terms of the Geneva Convention. As a result, hundreds of Waffen-SS officers were tried by the victorious Allies and sentenced to long prison terms for war crimes.

In the final analysis, the military professionalism, fighting spirit and *élan* of the Waffen-SS was not able to compensate for the overwhelming military supremacy of the Soviet Union. With Soviet tank production running at three times that of Germany, it was only a matter of time before the Eastern Front cracked. But it was not just a question of numbers (which has always been a convenient excuse for German failure). Stalin was also blessed with far more imaginative generals than Hitler. At several key points, the Russians clearly out-commanded the Germans, allowing them, for example, to defeat Operation Citadel and divert the Waffen-SS panzer divisions from the Kharkov front prior to the August 1943 Soviet summer offensive.

The war on the Eastern Front was a titanic struggle, but it has been much misunderstood in the West. Hopefully, this study has brought new light to bear on the battles of the Waffen-SS panzer divisions on the Eastern Front, which are often not given much prominence when compared to their actions in the West.

The war in the East moulded the Waffen-SS into the elite fighting force that caused the Western Allies so much trouble in Normandy in the summer of 1944, and later at Arnhem and in the Ardennes. The tactics and procedures pioneered on the Eastern Front by the Führer's 'Fire Brigade' proved a major shock to the

THE BITTER END

British and American armies when they landed on mainland Europe and faced the Waffen-SS panzers for the first time. The Western Allies were so impressed by these tactics that many were adopted after the war, and became the basis of NATO's battle plans to hold back any Soviet invasion of western Europe. Coming right up to date, the British Army, for example, has adopted the battle group as its standard combat unit, and the Americans used a version of the panzerkeil to batter through Iraqi defences during the 1991 Gulf War against Iraq.

Judged by the outcome of the war, the Waffen-SS panzer divisions failed in their mission. Germany was defeated. Their forays onto the battlefields of the Eastern Front, however, undoubtedly staved off a decisive defeat on more than one occasion. The intervention at Kharkov in February 1943 saved the Eastern Front, and probably extended the war by at least six months. The desperate battles around Kharkov in the autumn also prevented a major Soviet breakthrough that would have shortened the war considerably. Similarly, the counterattack at Zhitomir held together the Eastern Front for another four months. The role of the *Totenkopf* and *Wiking* Divisions in defending Warsaw in August and September of 1944 starkly illustrated the bitter fruits of victory by the Waffen-SS. Behind the steel shield of the Waffen-SS panzers, unimaginable slaughter and barbarity was allowed to reign unchecked. The Waffen-SS was truly the guardian of evil.

APPENDICES

Waffen-SS Ranks

SS-Oberstgruppenführer – Colonel-General
SS-Obergruppenführer – General
SS-Gruppenführer – Lieutenant-General
SS-Brigadeführer – Major-General
SS-Oberführer – Senior Colonel
SS-Standartenführer – Colonel
SS-Obersturmbannführer – Lieutenant-Colonel
SS-Sturmbannführer – Major
SS-Hauptsturmführer – Captain
SS-Obersturmführer – First Lieutenant
SS-Untersturmführer – Second Lieutenant
SS-Sturmscharführer – Senior Warrant Officer
SS-Hauptscharführer – Warrant Officer
SS-Oberscharführer – Staff Sergeant
SS-Scharführer – Sergeant
SS-Rottenführer – Corporal
SS-Sturmmann – Lance-Corporal
SS-Schütz – Private

APPENDICES

Waffen-SS Traditional Insignia

 1st SS Panzer Division *Leibstandarte*

 2nd SS Panzer Division *Das Reich*

 Das Reich Kursk marking

 3rd SS Panzer Division *Totenkopf*

 5th SS Panzer Division *Wiking*

 9th SS Panzer Division *Hohenstaufen*

 10th SS Panzer Division *Frundsberg*

 12th SS Panzer Division *Hitlerjugend*

Armoured Fighting Vehicle and Artillery Capabilities

German Panzer IIIJ
Type: Medium Tank
Designation: SdKfz 141
Weight: 24.8 tonnes (24.5 tons)
Speed: 41.6km/h (26mph)
Frontal Armour: 50mm (1.96in)
Gun: 50mm (able to penetrate T-34/76 side armour up to a range of 500m [1640ft])
Crew: Five
Range: 155km (97 miles)

German Panzer IVF/G
Type: Medium Tank
Designation: SdKfz 161
Weight: 24.3 tonnes (24 tons)
Speed: 40km/h (25mph)
Frontal Armour: 50mm (1.96in)
Gun: (able to penetrate T-34 armour up to a range of 2000m [6560ft])
Crew: Five
Range: 210km (131 miles)

German Panzer IVH
Type: Medium Tank
Designation: SdKfz 161/2
Weight: 25.4 tonnes (25 tons)
Speed: 40km/h (25mph)
Frontal Armour: 80mm (3.14in)
Gun: 75mm (able to penetrate T-34 armour up to a range of 2000m [6560ft] plus)
Crew: Five
Range: 210km (131 miles)

German Panther
Type: Heavy Medium Tank
Designation: SdKfz 171
Weight: 43.6 tonnes (43 tons)
Speed: 46.4km/h (29mph)
Frontal Armour: 100mm (3.93in)
Gun: 75mm (able to penetrate T-34 armour up to a range of 2000m [6560ft] plus)

APPENDICES

German Tiger I
Type: Heavy Tank
Designation: SdKfz 181
Weight: 57.9 tonnes (57 tons)
Speed: 38km/h (23mph)
Frontal Armour: 100mm (3.93in)
Gun: 88mm (able to penetrate T-34 armour up to a range of 2000m [6560ft] plus)
Crew: Five
Range: 140km (87 miles)

German Tiger II
Type: Heavy Tank
Designation: SdKfz 182
Weight: 69 tonnes (68 tons)
Speed: 35.2km/h (22mph)
Frontal Armour: 180mm (7in)
Gun: 88mm (able to penetrate T-34 armour up to a range of 2000m [6560ft] plus)
Crew: Five
Range: 170km (106 miles)

German Brummbär
Type: Assault Gun
Designation: StuG IV StuH43
Weight: 28.4 tonnes (28 tons)
Speed: 40km/h (28mph)
Frontal Armour: 100mm (3.93in)
Gun: 150mm
Crew: Five
Range: 210km (131 miles)

German Sturmgeschütz III
Type: Assault Gun
Designation: SdKfz 142/1
Weight: 26.4 tonnes (26 tons)
Speed: 40km/h (25mph)
Frontal Armour: 62mm (2.4in)
Gun: 75mm (able to penetrate T-34 armour up to a range of 2000m [6560ft])

German Marder III
Type: Self-Propelled Anti-tank Gun
Designation: Marder III
Weight: 11.1 tonnes (11 tons)

Speed: 41.6 km/h (26mph)
Frontal Armour: 25mm (.98in)
Gun: 76.2mm (able to penetrate T-34 armour up to a range of 1500m [4920ft])
Crew: Four
Range: 185km (116 miles)

German Jagdpanzer IV
Type: Self-Propelled Anti-tank Gun
Designation: SdKfz 162
Weight: 27.4 tonnes (27 tons)
Speed: 40km/h (25mph)
Frontal Armour: 80mm (3.14in)
Gun: 75mm (able to penetrate T-34 armour up to a range of 2000m [6560ft] plus)
Crew: Four
Range: 210km (131 miles)

German Jagdpanther
Type: Self-Propelled Anti-tank Gun
Designation: SdKfz 173
Weight: 46.7 tonnes (46 tons)

Speed: 46km/h (29mph)
Frontal Armour: 100mm (3.93in)
Gun: 88mm (able to penetrate T-34 armour up to a range of 2000m [6560ft] plus)
Crew: Five
Range: 160km (100 miles)

German Wespe
Type: Self-Propelled Howitzer
Designation: SdKfz 124
Weight: 13.3 tonnes (12.6 tons)
Speed: 40km/h (25mph)
Frontal Armour: 20mm (.78in)
Gun: 105mm (range 12.3km [7.6 miles])
Crew: Five
Range: 220km (137 miles)

German Hummel
Type: Self-Propelled Howitzer
Designation: SdKfz 165
Weight: 26.4 tonnes (26 tons)
Speed: 42km/h (26mph)

APPENDICES

Frontal Armour: 30mm
(1.18in)
Gun: 150mm (range 14km
[8.75 miles])
Crew: Five
Range: 215km (134 miles)

German SdKfz 251 SPW
Type: Armoured Personnel
Carrier
Designation: SdKfz 251
Weight: 9.5 tonnes (9.4 tons)
Speed: 41.6km/h (26mph)
Frontal Armour: 12mm
(.47in)
Gun: 2 x MG 42 machine
guns
Crew: Two
Range: 250km (156 miles)

**German 88mm Flak
(Antiaircraft) Gun**
Maximum Range: 16,200m
(53,150ft)
Rate of Fire: 15 rounds a
minute (able to penetrate
T-34 armour up to a range
of 2000m [6560ft] plus)

**German Nebelwerfer 42
Rocket Launcher**
Range: 7km (4.37 miles)
Tubes: 10

Soviet KV-1
Type: Heavy Tank
Designation: KV-1
Weight: 47.7 tonnes
(47 tons)
Speed: 33.6km/h (21mph)
Frontal Armour: 130mm
(5.1in)
Gun: 76mm (able to penetrate Panzer IV armour
up to a range of 1000m
[3280ft])
Crew: Five
Range: 150km (93 miles)

Soviet T-34/76
Type: Medium Tank
Designation: T-34/76
Weight: 33.5 tonnes
(33 tons)
Speed: 50km/h (31mph)
Frontal Armour: 80mm
(3.1in)
Gun: 76mm (able to penetrate Panzer IV armour up to

a range of 1000m [3280ft])
Crew: Four
Range: 186km (115 miles)

Soviet T-34/85
Type: Medium Tank
Designation: T-34/85
Weight: 35.5 tonnes (35 tons)
Speed: 55km/h (35mph)
Frontal Armour: 90mm (3.54in)
Gun: 85mm (able to penetrate Panther armour up to a range of 500m [1640ft])

Soviet 76.2mm Antitank Gun/Howitzer
Maximum Range: 13.9km (8.68 miles) (1000m [3280ft] direct fire)
Rate of Fire: 20 rounds a minute (able to penetrate Panzer IV armour up to a range of 1000m [3280ft])

Soviet SU-100
Type: Assault Gun
Designation: SU-100

Weight: 36.5 tonnes (36 tons)
Speed: 48km/h (30mph)
Frontal Armour: 45mm (1.7in)
Gun: 100mm (able to penetrate Panther armour up to a range of 5000m [16,404ft])
Crew: Four
Range: 240km (150 miles)

Orders of Battle

Glossary
Abteilung: battalion
Aufklärungs: reconnaissance
Flak: antiaircraft
Generalkommando: General Headquarters
Kompanie: company
Nachrichten: signals
Panzerjäger: antitank
Pioner: engineer
Sturm: assault
Wach: guard
Werfer: rocket artillery

I SS Panzer Corps' Order of Battle, 1943

Panzer Corps Headquarters (later II SS Panzer Korps)
SS-Panzer Abteilung 102/schw (heavy).
SS-Panzer Abteilung 502
(Tiger tanks from 1944)
Arko II. SS Panzer Corps/SS-Arko 102 (artillery command)
SS-Artillerie Abteilung 102
1. u. 2. SS-Gr. Werfer. Kompanie 102 (rocket)
SS-Flak Kompanie 102
SS-Werfer Abteilung. Generalkommando II.SS Panzer Corps/
 SS-Werfer Abteilung 102 (rockets)
Corps Nachr. Abteilung 400 (mot) (signals)

Leibstandarte Division
SS-Musik Corps LSSAH
SS-Panzergrenadier Regiment 1 *LSSAH*

SS-Panzergrenadier Regiment 2 LSSAH
SS-Panzer Regiment LSSAH 1
SS-Panzerjäger Abteilung LSSAH 1 (antitank)
SS-Sturmgeschütz Abteilung LSSAH 1
SS-Panzer Artillerie Regiment LSSAH 1
SS-Flak Abteilung LSSAH 1
SS-Werfer Abteilung LSSAH 1 (rocket)
SS-Panzer Nachrichten Abteilung LSSAH 1 (radio)
SS-Panzer Aufklärungs Abteilung LSSAH 1 (reconnaissance)
SS-Panzer Pioner Abteilung LSSAH 1 (combat engineer)
SS-Wach Abteilung (mot) LSSAH (often detached in Berlin for security work)

Das Reich Division
SS-Panzergrenadier Regiment 3 *Deutschland*
SS-Panzergrenadier Regiment *Der Führer*
SS-Infantry Regiment *Langemarck*
SS-Panzer Regiment 2
SS-Panzerjäger Abteilung 2 (antitank)
SS-Sturmgeschütz Abteilung 2
SS-Panzer Artillerie Regiment 2
SS-Flak Abteilung 2
SS-Werfer Abteilung 2 (rocket)
SS-Panzer Nachrichten Abteilung 2 (radio)
SS-Panzer Aufklärungs Abteilung 2 (reconnaissance)
SS-Panzer Pioner Battalion 2 (combat engineer)

Totenkopf Division
SS-Panzergrenadier Regiment 5 *Thule* (later titled *Totenkopf*)
SS-Panzergrenadier Regiment 6 *Theodor Eicke*

APPENDICES

SS-Panzer Regiment 3
SS-Panzerjäger Abteilung 3 (antitank)
SS-Sturmgeschütz Abteilung 3
SS-Panzer Artillerie Regiment 3
SS-Flak Abteilung 3
SS-Werfer Abteilung 3 (rocket)
SS-Panzer Nachrichten Abteilung 3 (radio)
SS-Panzer Aufklärungs Abteilung 3 (reconnaissance)
SS-Panzer Pioner Battalion 3 (combat engineer)

Wiking Division
SS-Panzergrenadier Regiment 9 *Germania*
SS-Panzergrenadier Regiment 10 *Westland*
SS-Panzergrenadier Regiment *Nordland* (left the division on 22 March 1943)
Estnisches SS-Freiwilligen Panzergrenadier Battalion Narwa (part of the division in the summer of 1943 and withdrawn in July 1944)
SS-Sturmbrigade *Wallonien* (temporarily attached in 1943–44)
SS-Panzer Regiment 5
SS-Panzerjäger Abteilung 5 (antitank)
SS-Sturmgeschütz Abteilung 5
SS-Panzer Artillerie Regiment 5
SS-Flak Abteilung 5
SS-Werfer Abteilung 5 (rocket)
SS-Panzer Nachrichten Abteilung 5 (radio)
SS-Panzer Aufklärungs Abteilung 5 (reconnaissance)
SS-Panzer Pioner Battalion 5 (combat engineer)

1./SS-Panzergrenadier Regiment 23 Norge *
1./SS-Panzergrenadier Regiment 24 Danmark *
SS-Panzer Abteilung Wiking (1942–43)

* These units were attached to the division in 1944–45

Army Group South Average Tank Strength, February 1943

XXXX Panzer Corps
3rd Panzer Division – 35 tanks
7th Panzer Division – 19 tanks
11th Panzer Division – 52 tanks
SS *Wiking* Division – 10 tanks

XXXXVIII Panzer Corps
17th Panzer Division – 6 tanks
6th Panzer Division – 17 tanks

SS Panzer Corps
SS *Leibstrandarte* Division – 37 tanks (including 3 Tiger Is)
SS *Das Reich* Division – 66 tanks (including 7 Tigers Is)
SS *Totenkopf* Division – 95 tanks (including 9 Tiger Is)

Army Detachment Kempf
Grossdeutschland Motorized Division – 103 tanks (including 4 Tiger Is)

Soviet Order of Battle in the Ukraine, February 1943

Third Tank Army
IV Tank Corps
XII Tank Corps
XV Tank Corps
8th Breakthrough Artillery Division
113th and 88th Tank Brigades
VI Guards Cavalry Corps
VII Guards Cavalry Corps
8 x rifle divisions

Sixth Army
I Guards Tank Corps
XXV Tank Corps
I Guards Cavalry Corps
15 x rifle divisions

First Guards Army
IV Guards Tank Corps*
III Tank Corps*
X Tank Corps*
XVIII Tank Corps*
14 x rifle divisions
2 x tank brigades
2 x rifle brigades

* assigned to Front Mobile Group Popov

II SS Panzer Corps' Order of Battle, July 1943

SS *Leibstrandarte* Division
SS *Das Reich* Division
SS *Totenkopf* Division
Artillery Command 122
1st Demonstration Rocket Regiment
52nd Rocket Regiment
2 x army artillery battalions
167th Infantry Division

Soviet Forces at Prokhorovka, 12 July 1943
Fifth Guards Army
XXXII Guards Rifle Corps
XXXIII Guards Rifle Corps
97th Guards Rifle Division
95th Guards Rifle Division
52nd Guards Rifle Division
42nd Guards Rifle Division
13th Guards Rifle Division
16th Guards Rifle Division
6th Guards Airborne Division
9th Guards Airborne Division
242nd Tank Brigade
237th Tank Brigade
99th Tank Brigade

APPENDICES

Fifth Guards Tank Army
XVIII Tank Corps (110th, 170th, 181st Tank, 32nd Guards Mechanized Brigades)
XXIX Tank Corps (25th, 31st, 32nd Tank, 53rd Mechanized Brigades)
V Guards Mechanized Corps (24th Guards Tank, 10th, 11th, 12th Guards Mechanized Brigades)

Fifty-Seventh Army
II Tank Corps (99th Guards, 26th Tank, 169th Tank , 58th Mechanized Brigades)
II Guards Tank Corps (4th, 25th, 26th Guards Tank Brigades, 4th Guards Mechanized Brigades)

German Sixth Army Order of Battle, July 1943
IV Corps
335th Infantry Division
3rd Mountain Division
304th Infantry Division
209th Assault Gun Brigade

XXIV Panzer Corps
3rd Panzer Division
23rd Panzer Division
16th Panzergrenadier Division
236th Assault Gun Brigade

II SS Panzer Corps
SS Das Reich Division
SS Totenkopf Division
1st Demonstration Rocket Regiment
52nd Rocket Regiment
6 x army artillery battalions

XVII Corps
302nd Infantry Division
306th Infantry Division
177th Infantry Division
294th Infantry Division

XXIX Corps
336th Infantry Division
17th Infantry Division
25th Luftwaffe Division
111th Infantry Division
243 Assault Gun Brigade

Soviet Order of Battle, Mius Front, July 1943
Second Guards Army
XXXI Guards Rifle Corps
   3 x rifle divisions

Fifth Shock Army
II Guards Mechanized Corps
IV Mechanized Corps (12, 13th 15th Mechanized Brigades)
   32nd Tank Brigade
   8th Anti-Tank Brigade
I Guards Rifle Corps
   9 x rifle divisions
   6 x rocket regiments

Twenty-Eighth Army
XIII Guards Rifle Corps
   7 x rifle divisions
   1 x tank brigades

APPENDICES

German Forces in the Kharkov Sector, August 1943
III Panzer Corps (west of Kharkov)
3rd Panzer Division
SS Wiking Division
SS Das Reich Division
SS Totenkopf Division
34th Infantry Division
223rd Infantry Division

IX Corps (defence of Kharkov)
3rd Panzer Division
6th Panzer Division
SS *Das Reich* Division (relocated)
106th Infantry Division
168th Infantry Division
198th Infantry Division
320th Infantry Division
248th Infantry Division

Soviet Order of Battle West of Kharkov, August 1943
Sixth Guards Tank Army
V Guards Tank Corps (20th, 21st, 22nd Guards Tank Brigades, 6th Guards Motorized Brigade)
XXIII Rifle Corps (51st, 52nd, 20th Guards Rifle Divisions)
XXII Guards Rifle Corps (67th, 71st, 90th Guards Rifle Divisions)

First Tank Army
VI Tank Corps (200th, 112th, 22nd Tank Brigades, 6th Motorized Brigade)

III Mechanized Corps (1st, 3rd and 10th Mechanized Brigades, 49th Tank and 1st Guards Tank Brigades)
XXXI Tank Corps (100th, 237th and 242nd Tank Brigades) 13th Rifle Division
XXXII Guards Rifle Corps (66th, 97th, 136th Guards Rifle Divisions, 93rd Tank Brigade)

Fifth Guards Tank Army
V Guards Mechanized Corps (10th, 11th and 12th Mechanized Brigades)
XVIII Tank Corps (110th, 170th and 181st Tank Brigades, 32nd Motorized Brigades)
XXIX Tank Corps (25th, 31st and 32nd Tank Brigades, 53rd Motorized Brigades)
XXXIII Guards Rifle Corps (66th, 96th Rifle Division, 9th Guards Airborne Division)

German XXXXIV Panzer Corps' Order of Battle, November 1943
SS *Leibstandarte* Division
1st Panzer Division
7th Panzer Division
19th Panzer Division
25th Panzer Division
68th Infantry Division
Kampfgruppe SS *Das Reich* Division

German Order of Battle, Cherkassy Pocket, February 1944

The Rescue Force
III Panzer Corps
  SS *Leibstandarte* Division
  1st Panzer Division
  6th Panzer Division
  16th Panzer Division
  17th Panzer Division
  Heavy Panzer Regiment Bake
  249th Assault Gun Brigade
  54th Rocket Regiment

Operating in support of Rescue Force
XLVII Panzer Corps
  3rd Panzer Division
  11th Panzer Division
  13th Panzer Division
  14th Panzer Division
  106th Infantry Division
  282nd Infantry Division
  320th Infantry Division
  911st Assault Gun Brigade

In the Pocket
XLII Corps
  88th Infantry Division
  417th Infantry Regiment
  Kamfgruppe B (elements of the 112th 332nd and 255th Infantry Divisions)
  805 Assault Gun Brigade

XI Corps
SS *Wiking* Division
  SS Walloon Assault Brigade
  57th Infantry Division
  72nd Infantry Division
  389th Infantry Division
  202 Assault Gun Brigade
  GHQ Light Artillery Battalion

Hohenstaufen and *Frundsberg* Divisions Orders of Battle

Hohenstaufen Division
SS-Panzergrenadier Regiment 19
SS-Panzergrenadier Regiment 20
SS-Panzer Regiment 9
SS-Panzerjäger Abteilung 9 (antitank)
SS-Sturmgeschütz Abteilung 9
SS-Panzer Artillerie Regiment 9
SS-Flak Abteilung 9
SS-Flak Kompanie
SS-Panzer Nachrichten Abteilung 9 (radio)
SS-Panzer Aufklärungs Abteilung 9 (reconnaissance)
SS-Panzer Pioner Battalion 9 (combat engineer)

Frundsberg Division
SS-Panzergrenadier Regiment 21
SS-Panzergrenadier Regiment 22
SS-Panzer Regiment 10
SS-Panzerjäger Abteilung 10 (antitank)
SS-Sturmgeschütz Abteilung 10

SS-Panzer Artillerie Regiment 10
SS-Flak Abteilung 10
SS-Panzer Nachrichten Abteilung 10 (radio)
SS-Panzer Aufklärungs Abteilung 10 (reconnaissance)
SS-Panzer Pionier Abteilung 10 (combat engineer)

I SS Panzer Corps *LSSAH* and *Hitlerjugend* Orders of Battle

I SS Panzer Corps *Leibstandarte* Adolf Hitler
schw. (heavy) SS-Panzer Abteilung 101/501 (Tiger tanks from 1944)
SS-Arko I (artillery command)
SS-Artillerie Abteilung 101; renamed schw. SS-(Corps-) Artillerie-Abteilung 501
SS-Flak Abteilung 101
SS-Flak Kompanie
SS-Werfer Brigade I. (rockets)
SS-Werfer Abteilung 101/501 (rockets)
SS-Vielfachwerferbatterie (mot) 522 (rockets)
SS-Korps Nachrichten Abteilung 101/501 (radio)

Hitlerjugend Division
SS-Panzergrenadier Regiment 25
SS-Panzergrenadier Regiment 26
SS-Panzer Regiment 12
Army's Panzer Jagerg Abteilung 560 (antitank)
SS-Panzerjäger Abteilung 12 (antitank)
SS-Sturmgeschütz Abteilung 12
SS-Panzer Artillerie Regiment 12
SS-Flak Abteilung 12
SS-Werfer Abteilung 12 (rockets)

SS-Panzer Nachrichten Abteilung 12 (radio)
SS-Panzer Aufklärungs Abteilung 12 (reconnaissance)
SS-Pioneer Battalion 12
SS-Panzer Pioner Battalion 12 (combat engineer)

BIBLIOGRAPHY

Brett-Smith, Richard, *Hitler's Generals*, Osprey, London, 1976
Carell, Paul, *Scorched Earth*, Ballantine, New York, 1971
Cooper, Matthew and Lucas, James, *Panzer*, Macdonald, London, 1976
Cooper, Matthew and Lucas, James, *Panzergrenadier*, Macdonald and Jane's, London, 1977
Cooper, Matthew and Lucas, James, *Hitler's Elite*, Grafton, London, 1990
Clark, Alan, *Barbarossa*, William Morrow, New York, 1965
Cross, Robin, *Citadel: The Battle of Kursk*, Michael O'Mara, London, 1993
Downing, David, *The Devils Virtuosos*, New English Library, London, 1976
Dunnigan, James, *The Russian Front*, Arms and Armour, London, 1978
Edwards, Roger, *Panzer: A Revolution in Warfare, 1939-45*, Arms and Armour, London, 1989
Erickson, John, *The Road to Berlin*, Weidenfeld & Nicolson, London, 1983
Glantz, David, *From the Don to the Dnieper*, Frank Cass, London, XXXX
Guderian, Heinz, *Panzer Leader*, Futura, London, 1979
Forty, George, *German Tanks of World War Two*, Blandford Press, London, 1987
Jentz, Thomas, Doyle, Hilary and Sarson, Peter, *Tiger I*, Osprey, London, 1993

Jentz, Thomas, *Panzer Truppen*, Schiffer Military History, Atglen, 1996

Kessler, Leo, *The Iron Fist*, Futura, London, 1977

Kleine, Egon and Kuhn, Volkmar, *Tiger*, Motorbuch Verlag, Stuttgart

Lehman, Rudolf, *The Leibstandarte*, JJ Fedorowicz, Manitoba, 1990

Lucas, James, *Grossdeutschland*, London, 1978

Manstein, Erich von, *Lost Victories*, Methuen, London, 1958

Mellenthin, F.W., *Panzer Battles*, Futura, London, 1977

Mitchell, Samuel, *Hitler's Legions*, Leo Cooper, London, 1985

Nipe, George, *Decision in the Ukraine*, JJ Fedorowicz, Manitoba, 1996

Reynolds, Michael, *Men of Steel*, Spellmount, Staplehurst, 1999

Rotmistrov, Pavel, *Tanks against Tanks*

Sadarananda, Dana, *Beyond Stalingrad*, Praeger, New York, 1990

Seaton, Albert, *The Russo-German War, 1941-45*, Praeger, New York, 1970

Senger und Etterlin, General Fridio von, *Neither Fear nor Hope*, Greenhill, London, 1989

Snydor, Charles, *Soldiers of Destruction: The SS Totenkopf Division 1933-45*, Princeton University, 1977

Spaeter, Helmuth, *Die Einsatze der Panzergrenadier-division Grossdeutschland*, Podzun-Pallas-Verlag, 1986

Soviet General Staff: The Battle for Kursk 1943 (eds. Glantz, David and Orenstein, Harold), Frank Cass, London, 1999

BIBLIOGRAPHY

Stadler, Silvester, *Die Offensive gegen Kursk 1943*, Munin Verlag, Osnabruck, 1980

Ziemke, Earle, *Stalingrad to Berlin*, US Government Printing Office, Washington, DC, 1968

Records of the Wehrmacht Inspector of Panzer Troops

War Diary of XXXXVIII Panzer Corps, December 1943

German Reports Series, 18 Volumes, US Army

www.ingramcontent.com/pod-product-compliance
Lightning Source LLC
Chambersburg PA
CBHW051751040426
42446CB00007B/321